Please
Tell Me How
You Feel

Please Tell Me How You Feel

MARION STROUD

BETHANY HOUSE PUBLISHERS
MINNEAPOLIS, MINNESOTA 55438
A Division of Bethany Fellowship, Inc.

Originally published in Great Britain under the title,
Knowing Me, Knowing You.

Copyright © 1982
Marion Stroud
All Rights Reserved

Published by Bethany House Publishers
A Division of Bethany Fellowship, Inc.

Printed in the United States of America

Library of Congress Cataloging in Publication Data

Stroud, Marion.
    Please tell me how you feel.

    Originally published under title: Knowing me,
knowing you.
    Bibliography: p.
    1. Interpersonal communication. I. Title.
BF637.C45S85   1984   153.6   83–22410
ISBN 0–87123–427–0 (pbk.)

Contents

NB The reader will find the full bibliographical references
to the titles followed by a ★ in the Bibliography

The Gift of Words

Thank you, God, for teaching us to talk to one another.
Thank you for the gift of words.
Thank you for giving us each other with whom to share our
hopes, our fears, our problems and our plans.

Thank you for that assurance, that since there is no fear in
love, we can be totally honest, completely ourselves, without the risk of ridicule or rejection.

Thank you for showing us the need to listen. To listen with
our hearts as well as with our ears. To sense the needs that
may remain unspoken beneath a torrent of words. And to
know that when there are no words to meet the situation,
then love can be a silent song — a touch that says 'I'm in
this situation with you', a smile that reassures 'You're doing
fine'.

Thank you that we have learned the need for patience. The
discipline to talk things through until both minds are satisfied. Even if we then return to the original solution!
Thank you for teaching a talkative partner brevity, and a
quieter one how to express himself.

Thank you, God, for teaching us to talk to one another.
Thank you for the gift of words. (*The Gift of Marriage*,★
Lion Publ.)

Introduction

'Come with me, and let us learn this language of love together. For it is only when I openly and honestly share my thoughts, my longings, my dreams and my fears with you — at the same time working to understand yours, so that I can fulfil your needs — that real communication takes place.'

'Why is it that so many people seem to spend so much of the time misunderstanding each other?' sighed Leonie, as we stood at the school gates waiting for our children to come tumbling through the cloakroom doors. 'I think that I must have offended Ann again. She looked straight through me in the butcher's just now. And I've only just sorted out what it was that I said to upset her last month. I always seem to be putting my foot in it with someone.'

'I think that it's about time that we had an "International Year of Better Understanding". Let's see . . . how does the "Year of Interpersonal Communication" grab you?' suggested Claire. (Claire is our learned friend. Leonie reckons that she eats a page from the dictionary instead of toast for breakfast!) 'After all,' she went on, 'it seems ridiculous that we can talk on the telephone to people on the other side of the world, and television tells us what is going on there almost as soon as it happens, and yet we are so bad at getting what we really mean across to our own family and friends.'

'And it's a problem for most people in one way or another,' observed Helen. 'Marcia was on the phone at 7.30 this morning in floods of tears, because she and John have hardly spoken all weekend. Today, he's gone abroad on a business trip and she still doesn't know what is causing the trouble. It seems as if he can't talk about it — or maybe it's just that he won't — and so Marcia can't do anything to put things right.'

'That's the point,' chimed in Sue. 'This communication business is a two-way thing. I reckon that after seeing that TV programme on Saturday I know more about the problems and habits of the wandering herdsmen of Outer Mongolia East, than I do about my next door neighbours. That little rose hedge between our gardens might as well be a twenty foot high wall. It's almost as if they've dug a moat around themselves, and although I want to get to know them, I don't know how to find the drawbridge. There's about as much life in our relationship as there is in Mike Morrison's parrot!'

'What on earth has a parrot got to do with anything?' I queried quite bewildered.

'Oh, haven't you heard about the Morrison brothers?' Sue asked, with a mischievous twinkle in her eyes.

'No.'

'Go on!'

'Do tell us,' we urged her, anxious to hear the rest of the story before the school bell rang.

'Well,' she said, 'every year these two tried to outdo each other in finding really original presents to give to their parents at Christmas. One year Mike heard that his brother was giving his parents tickets for a world cruise, and that really floored him. There seemed to be no way of topping a gift like that. Then, as he was passing a pet shop, Mike saw a parrot in the window with a price label of one thousand pounds on its cage. He went into the shop and asked the assistant why there was such a fantastic price on the bird.

'Abdul is a very rare parrot, Sir! Worth every penny,' the assistant assured him. 'He can speak ten languages fluently.'

Delighted, Mike bought the parrot and arranged for Abdul to be delivered to his parents. He was convinced that the honours for originality would certainly be his that year.

He could hardly wait for Christmas Day to come so that he could telephone and find out how they liked his gift.

'Mother!' he said, 'how did you like the bird?'

'It was delicious, dear,' she assured him.

'Delicious,' Mike bellowed. 'Mother, Abdul was unique . . . he cost me one thousand pounds and spoke ten languages.'

There was a horrified silence at the other end of the phone.

'I'm very sorry, Mike,' apologised his mother eventually, 'but if he was so clever, why didn't he say something? I don't think that he could have spoken English, dear, because he didn't say anything that I could understand. If he had, of course, things would have been very different.'

'Poor old Abdul!' I thought, still chuckling inwardly at Sue's tall story as we wended our way home. He could speak ten languages fluently, but he didn't say anything that his new owner could understand. If he had, things would have been very different. As it was, he ended up in the oven.

Of course, there aren't too many multi-lingual parrots around, nor misguided mothers with exotic tastes in cookery, but that silly story is a picture of real-life situations which are being repeated day after day, all over the world. Relationships which are bursting with the potential for fun, interest and companionship never get off the ground — or worse still, wither and die — because we find it so hard to discover the right way to express ourselves, so that the other person can really understand us and we them. And as a result nations go to war with words and with weapons; bosses and workers work against rather than for each other, and, on a more intimate level, marriages fall apart, family relationships are strained and soured and friendships become formalities.

I thought back to snippets of conversations that I had had with people in previous weeks:

'Jim and I have been married for twenty years and I think that I know less about how he really thinks and feels now, than before we were married,' Margaret had said sadly. 'Life is so hectic: we don't seem to have time to talk anymore.'

'I couldn't possibly tell my parents that I want to leave college half way through my course,' Sarah had sobbed. 'They would think that I was letting them down. They would never understand!'

'Mrs Atkinson has handed in her resignation,' the chairman of the committee had announced. 'She says that she is too busy to continue but I'm rather afraid that that is not the real reason.'

'Do you think that the ability to communicate — you know, being able to talk openly and honestly and really understand other people is something you're born with, like red hair or a good singing voice?' I wondered aloud. 'Or is it a skill that can be taught and that anyone can learn?'

Leonie shrugged. 'It seems to me that if you are totally honest with someone, either you get hurt or they do,' she said with a sigh. 'If there's a way to communicate without that happening, then I could do with a crash course.'

'Perhaps we all need to learn another language,' suggested Claire. 'I don't mean just another way of saying things, but developing a kind of sixth sense which would help us to react in the right way to a particular person in a given situation, and which would mean that we would know how to listen as well as how to speak. If only we could learn to do that it would solve an awful lot of problems.'

So ended a casual conversation which didn't seem very important at the time. But that afternoon chat became the starting point for this book, when I decided — quite idly at first — to try and discover whether anyone knew if there was such a thing as this 'special language' which Claire had talked about, and whether it could be learned, or was just the birthright of the fortunate few. After long months of talking, listening, reading and researching (and getting more and more fascinated by the whole subject) I bring you the good news! *Communication is a skill that can be learned by anyone of any age, anywhere!* The strong and silent (or mild and mousey) types can do it as well as the nineteen-to-the dozen talkers, for there are many ways of communicating. Obviously some people find it easier than others.

Certainly there are plenty of pitfalls and problems that will not disappear overnight (or even, perhaps, in the space of weeks or months). But the fact remains that if you feel that your communication rating is lower than you would like it to be — whether with your marriage partner, children, relations or friends — it *can* be improved.

In his book *The Secret of Staying in Love** John Powell says, 'The genius of communication is the ability to be totally honest and totally kind at the same time.' If you want to be a genius, there are just two major pre-requisites: an open heart, open ears and eyes, and a willingness to give time and thought to learning what is, in the very widest sense of the words 'a language of love'.

1: Turn Your Radio On

'We communicate with all kinds of people, for all sorts of reasons, in various ways, and on many different levels.'

It was a 'must'; a 'have-to'; one of those things that no self-respecting tourist should miss. 'Take the canoe across the lake!' they told us. 'You'll just love the Indian paintings on the rocks by the north shore. It's really neat the way those Indians could tell a story with just a few strokes of an old horse hair brush. The water is calm; you're wearing your life-jackets — there'll be no problems! Have a nice trip.'

It sounded very simple, the way they put it, and so, full of misplaced confidence, we paddled out into the deep. But what we were *not* told was that there was no beach by the rock paintings and that for inexpert canoeists to try to get a closer look by endeavouring to land on the rocks was asking for a capsize. Well, we asked for it and we got it — an icy dip in an extremely deep Canadian lake and a very quick and distorted view of the paintings!

We proved that day that canoes are trickier things to handle than it might appear to the casual observer, and that getting a good view of those paintings was not the picnic that we had been led to believe that it would be!

The same can definitely be said about charting a straight-forward passage through the wide-open waters of 'Lake Communication' and struggling to find a safe landing point on its rocky shores. While we are trying to get a clear picture of the 'how' and the 'why' of such an enormous and technical subject, we can very easily get tipped out into the chilly waters of complicated theories, and unintelligible theses! So perhaps we had better take a tip from those Indian artists and be content with sketching in the bare bones of the story as we look for the answers to three very basic questions —

What is communication and who needs it anyway?

If I need it, how do I get it?

Where do I go wrong?

What is communication?

According to my pocket Oxford Dictionary, 'Communication is the imparting or exchange of news, discovery, information or feeling' and, in spite of all the difficulties it leads us into, we can't get along without it! After all, right back in the beginning of history God saw that Adam needed someone to share things with and so he gave him a partner, and there was total openness between man and woman and God. That was real communication!

Then came rebellion and disobedience and the need for the first 'cover-up' — and we've had problems in relationships ever since! But the basic need to communicate, or, to put it another way to love and share our lives with others, is built into our very nature by God.

There is, of course, much more to communication than the type of conversation that you might hear at the church door on any Sunday morning. You know the kind of thing:

' 'Morning Dave, how are you?'
'Fine, thanks.'
'How's the wife?'
'Fine.'
'And little Pete?'
'Fine.'
'Mother-in-law better now?'
'Yes, she's fine!'
when in actual fact, if you went home with Dave you might well find that he was worried sick about a possible redundancy; his wife was having a fit of the monthly blues, little Pete had a sleep problem and mother-in-law wasn't speaking to any of them!

This is what is known as 'Cliché Level Conversation', and as we can see, it keeps right away from personal sharing and is very superficial. In his book *'Why I am afraid to tell you who I am'* John Powell describes five levels of communication, putting 'Cliché Level Conversation' at Level five —

Level Four is 'Reporting the facts about others';

Level Three is 'My Ideas and Judgements';

Level Two is 'My Feelings and Emotions';

Level One is 'Complete and Personal Communication'.

Let's think how the conversation with Dave might change if he became more open in his sharing.

'Morning, Dave, how are you?'

'Oh! Not too bad, I suppose!' (Level 5)

'You look a bit down in the dumps! How's the family?'

'Don't ask! We're going through a difficult patch with Pete at the moment. He's just not sleeping. Mother-in-law is better in health but worse in temper and everything is getting on top of Molly – she's really worn out.' (Level 4)

'Oh! That's tough! What can we do to help?'

'I don't know. I think I really need to take a day or two's holiday and give Molly a real break, but with the job situation as it is, it's too risky to take time off. (Level 3) Quite frankly, I'm worried sick about our firm, and with things at home going from bad to worse I feel as if I'm in a long, dark tunnel and there's no way out.' (Level 2, moving towards Level 1.)

15

At that point Dave would almost certainly stop, for we rarely mention our deepest problems and needs if there is any chance of being overheard, and a wise friend would take him somewhere more private than the church porch to continue the conversation, or offer to meet him for a more personal chat later.

Which of the two conversations do you think would benefit Dave most? In the long term, it would be the one in which he really opens his heart, because, although it is costly to our pride to admit that all is not well with us, that we can't cope and that we need the help and support of others, the very act of sharing our problems and fears honestly with someone we can trust is a therapy in itself. The old proverb, 'A problem shared is a problem halved' has a great deal of truth in it.

If I need to communicate, how do I do it?

During the first weeks of its life, a baby has one means of communication — a cry! A baby cries when it is hungry, and it cries when it is uncomfortable or lonely or bored. Even the most amateur of mothers soon begins to pick out the various tones in that one sound and to interpret what the baby means — most of the time, anyway! As the child grows he develops other skills until as an adult he is communicating with the world around him in many different ways. But whether it is Baby or Grandpa who wants to make his needs known, communication still takes place in the same way — there must be a person with a message to give; the message and a person receiving the message, or, to put it in more concise terms, *a transmitter, a message* and *a receiver*.

In order to get a slightly more detailed picture of how the communication process works, and the problems that we run into, let's imagine that I am finding that there is more month than there is housekeeping money (a not uncommon experience!) and I decide to let my husband know about it, because I want his help in sorting things out. This is the *purpose* of my message.

On this occasion, I become *the transmitter* and he becomes

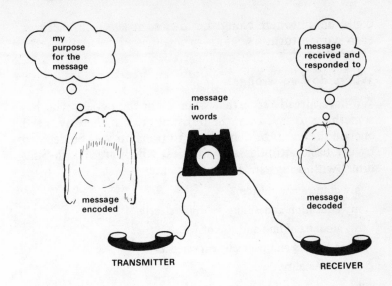

my
purpose
for the
message

message
received and
responded to

message
in
words

message
encoded

message
decoded

TRANSMITTER

RECEIVER

the receiver. Although he understands me pretty well, he can't read my thoughts, and so I have to decide how to put him in the picture. I decide that a SERIOUS TALK would be the best way to do it and so I have to *encode* my thoughts into words, and they then become the *message.*

Those words travel via sound waves through the air to my husband's ears; he *decodes* the message, understands the bad news that I am trying to give him and (hopefully!) offers me a loan, agrees to live on baked beans until pay-day or makes some other helpful suggestion! If that happens, my purpose has been accomplished and communication is said to have taken place.

'Aha!' you might say, 'but what about the times when you speak, your husband listens and then responds, but in quite the wrong way? Is that communication? And who has got it wrong? Is it you; is it him, or is it the message that is at fault?

There is not an easy answer to that! But it seems obvious that if he hasn't received what I wanted to share, then I haven't communicated effectively. The break-down point

17

could lie anywhere along the line, so it is worth checking each part in turn.

Where do I go wrong?

We have already seen that when I am the person who has something to say, I am the transmitter. But the way that I encode the message that I have to transmit will be decided by my basic attitudes and abilities, which are like in-built filters within myself. These filters are —

my culture and customs

my education and ability to think clearly

my understanding and use of words

my attitudes and previous experiences

my personality.

When we think about it, it is pretty obvious, isn't it? The culture and family customs in which we have grown up, colour and shape our whole attitude to life. Then there is education. Ideally this should teach a person to think clearly, and so a highly-educated person would be more likely to be able to think through problems logically and express them clearly, than someone who has had little formal training. And of course, the personality with which we were born, and the experiences that we have had over the years, all play a part in deciding the way in which we view ourselves and other people. But that is only one part of the problem. Not only does my message have to pass through these filters, but like a transmitter of the more mechanical variety, I can develop faults. These faults occur when I fail to —

pin-point my purpose

encode the message accurately or

choose the appropriate medium for the message.

Tuning the transmitter

If I don't have a clear idea of what I am trying to say, it will hardly be surprising if the receiver gets a distorted signal! So, especially when there is a sensitive subject under discussion, I need to pin-point my message, thinking before I speak, and trying to express myself clearly and accurately (easy to say now, in cold blood, but much harder to do in the heat of the moment!).

This brings us to *accurate encoding*. The words I choose and the way I say them are very important. There is many a misunderstanding that takes place at this point! Think about my financial crisis again for a moment. There are many ways in which I could approach the problem and try to put my message across. Here are just four of them.

1. (When you know that this is not the case.) 'Are you sure that you gave me *all* the housekeeping for this month? My purse seems pretty light. Or is it just that you haven't paid me back for filling the car with petrol?'

2. 'I heard on the radio today that the average weekly shop for a family like ours costs £1.20 more now than it did three months ago. Imagine that! It doesn't sound to me as if this government is doing much about inflation!'

3. 'Do you know, Dick is really mean with money. Margo only gets £20 a week housekeeping, and they've got all those children! He just takes advantage of the fact that she's a marvellous manager. Mind you, she was a school teacher and they can always add up, can't they? Not like me; I'm hopeless with money!'

4. 'I'm afraid all the visitors that we've had this month have made a real dent in the budget. Is the "Rainy Day Fund" likely to be able to bridge the gap until Friday? Or will we just have to tighten our belts and eat beans?'

How will the poor man decode messages one, two and three? With message No 1 he might well get very angry because it seems as if I am trying to shift the responsibility for the problem onto his shoulders, quite unjustly. He may take message No 2 as an invitation to give me a lecture on the Government's financial policies, and with message No 3 he may simply wish that he had married Margo instead of me! Message No 4 which talks about the problem and solutions as I see them, but is open to another suggestion from him is the permutation that is most likely to deliver the goods in our house — how about yours?

Choose the right medium for the message

There are three main ways in which we express ourselves — through our words, through our actions and through our senses and emotions. Surprising though it may seem, the experts tell us that we don't talk as much as we think that we do, for 70% of our communication is carried out without words. So although we have thought of the message in terms of words up until now (and that is probably the best choice for this particular situation), there *are* other options. Supposing that I decided that I couldn't possibly talk to my husband about such a thorny subject as money. I might decide to *do* something (such as serving up baked beans for dinner for the next three nights) and hope that he would take the hint. Then I would be encoding the message into actions, but the decoding of the message (in this instance and in all others) would depend very much on the receptivity of the receiver.

The receptivity of the receiver

Just as the transmitter has in-built filters, so does the receiver. The message is decoded through these filters and there is always a degree of blurring or distortion. An expanded communication diagram would look like this:

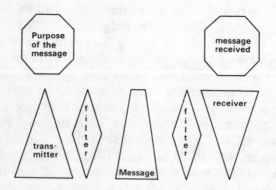

Let's think about those baked beans as our 'message through actions'. In our family of seven people, three members actively like baked beans, two regard them as so-so, and two loathe them. So instead of conveying anything about money, three nights of baked bean dinners might well be interpreted as a treat by the bean-freaks, a bore by the neutrals and a positive insult by the bean-haters. You see, their attitude to baked beans would act as a filter to their understanding of my message! And the real idea that I was trying to convey might be considerably delayed in reachings its target, or filtered out altogether because I had chosen the wrong medium for my message and had not considered the receptivity of the receiver.

Faults and filters in transmitter and receiver and mistakes in the message — these are some of the main reasons why our communication with each other is blurred or breaks down, but there is still one other major group of obstacles which can bend or block our signals. These are the barriers we raise to protect ourselves from unwelcome or threatening messages. We'll get to grips with these in the next chapter.

2: Man the Barricades!

'People are lonely because they build walls instead of bridges.'

'Mary Jane, I'm telling thee now that I love thee,' said Joshua, a young man more at home with sheep than with people, on his wedding day. 'I don't hold with repeating myself so I shan't tell thee again, but if I have any cause to change my mind I'll let thee know about it!' And with that expression of his feelings Mary Jane had to be content for the next fifty years! I can't help thinking that the charms of the strong and silent variety of male, so beloved by writers of romantic fiction are distinctly over-rated!

I wonder if Mary Jane ever felt lonely in her marriage? We often fall into the trap of thinking that the only lonely people are single people. But this is by no means so. Loneliness is not left at the church door with the confetti and rose petals. A man and a woman can live in the same house — in fact they can lie side by side in the same bed, and still be emotionally miles apart, unable to share their lives on any more than the most superficial level because they have retreated behind carefully constructed barricades rather than risking the perils and pleasures of effective bridge building.

I don't feel the need to communicate	I don't recognise your needs	I don't like the way you communicate	It's too much effort	I'm too tired
I don't want to change my ideas or viewpoints	I know all about you anyway		I'm too busy with work or household duties	I'm not interested in enabling you to change
I've heard		we'll communicate my way or not at all	there are some things better left unsaid	
I AM AFRAID TO TELL YOU WHO I AM				

'This marriage business is just one big confidence trick,' wept one disillusioned young wife. 'They say that it is all a matter of give and take and so it is — I give and my husband takes! Every night it's the same. He comes in, eats his meal and then retires behind the paper, switches on the television or gets on with the work that he has brought home. We talk so little that I sometimes wonder whether he's taken a vow of silence! And yet before we were married we always had so much to say. Is it me, is it him, or is it marriage that is killing our communication stone dead? We still love each other but I wonder how long our love can last in this atmosphere. What is happening to us?'

What indeed? Why *do* we shy away from each other when deep down each one of us has the need to be close to at least one other person: to love and to be loved: to know and to be completely known and accepted for what we are. The barriers behind which we withdraw are as many and as varied in detailed design as the people who build them, but there seems to be two main reasons why we choose barricades rather than bridges.

1. We fail to understand the importance of real communication.

2. We are afraid of the consequences that might come in the wake of really honest sharing.

'I don't feel the need to communicate.'

'The main trouble with women,' said Alec, stretching his legs out towards the fire, 'is that you all love to talk, whereas we men are much more self-contained!' A stunned silence greeted this sweeping statement, and he hurriedly took advantage of it! 'When I get home in the evening, I like to hear what Jenny has been doing of course, but I don't usually want to indulge in in-depth analysis about my feelings on this subject or my reactions to that thorny problem. I've been arguing my case and hearing the other fellow's point of view all day at work, and I'm too tired to start again when I get home. One of our big difficulties is that Jenny can never make a decision quickly! She always has to look at things from a dozen different angles, and discuss every aspect of the problem at great length, whereas I usually opt for the obvious solution. And that is the one that we generally end up with, however much we beat about the bush beforehand. But Jenny's method wastes so much time! Who needs these great heart-to-hearts? My parents never seemed to have them and they got along all right.'

Jenny bit her lip and refrained from pointing out to Alec, what she had already told me — that her husband's mother, Nan, had once confided in her that she and Alec's father were emotional strangers, and that Nan had felt that she was the loneliest lady in town. Jenny had no wish to walk the same road as her mother-in-law, but in the face of Alec's apparent lack of any need for in-depth sharing, she was at a loss to know how to make her own needs known.

Alec was not a particularly selfish person; indeed he was active in his church and community, and regarded by his work-mates as a kind and considerate sort. But, like many of us, he viewed the world largely from his own stand-point. Instead of seeing Jenny as an individual, with her own needs (and faults and failings) he fell into the trap of generalising about the opposite sex and expecting Jenny to fit in with his pre-conceived ideas about women, marriage, and what constituted a 'normal' relationship. Alec, in common with many men, said that he felt no need for in-depth communication with his wife because he received all that he needed in the way of mental stimulation from other people. He had never been inclined to talk much about his feelings anyway for he was naturally a fairly reserved person. In addition to this, at the end of the working day, he was too tired to make the effort to do something which he had never been taught to regard as important by his own parents (and which he secretly feared might lead him into an emotionally uncomfortable position). Culture, customs, experience and personality act as barriers to communication as well as filters through which the message must pass! And yet, if anyone had suggested that he did not love Jenny he would have been deeply hurt and upset. Perhaps Alec had forgotten (or maybe never realised) that love in action is ready to give up its own comfort and convenience, and to invest time, thought and energy in meeting the other's needs and enabling the loved one to grow and develop as a person. At any rate, it was when he faced up to the fact that, irrespective of his own needs, Jenny needed to communicate, and that it was his responsibility to meet that need of hers (at least in part) that their problems began to resolve themselves.

Ian and Elinor had a different row of bricks in their barricade! They had been married for many years, and had slipped into that deceptive and dangerous habit of thinking that they knew all there was to know about each other and that there was nothing new to discover. Ian was one of those people who had thought out what he believed, what he wanted from life and why, in his late teens, and as far as he was concerned that was that for all time. He was extremely busy in his very responsible job and deeply committed to his leadership responsibilities within the large church in which he and Elinor worshipped, and he liked his life just as it was — comfortable, secure and in a rut! For a long time he didn't notice that his wife was slowly but surely changing as her family responsibilities decreased, and she was able to give more time to developing her own identity and to the discovery of new skills and fresh interests. When he did, he felt short-changed and cheated. He refused to discuss some of the new ideas and insights about love and life and their relationship that she wanted to raise with him, because he wasn't willing to be convinced or to change his point of view.

Eventually, Ian's insistence on 'communication-on-my terms and in-my-time' — which in practice meant hardly ever — and his reluctance to see Elinor as a growing, changing and expanding personality, instead of a stereotyped 'Chief Executive's Wife' meant that their communication dwindled away, and their marriage withered and almost died. Ian discovered the hard way that neglect and indifference are just as threatening to a relationship as any of the more obvious dangers. He also had to face the fact that to create 'no-go' areas in a marriage because we are afraid to discuss them may give a temporary feeling of security, but it is security that is really an illusion, built as it is on a foundation of fear.

Why am I afraid to tell you who I am?

In his book of that title John Powell answers his own question in this way. 'If I tell you who I am, you may not like who I am, and that is all that I have.' This is the root cause of all our barrier building. If I let you get close to me and open my heart to you with no holding back, I place myself in your hands and arm you with a weapon of knowledge that you can use to hurt me very deeply. It seems perfectly reasonable then to be afraid. But these fears are such effective saboteurs of real closeness, sharing and understanding that if we refuse to face up to them they have great power to bind and imprison us. So we have a choice. We can stay safely behind our barricades and find that our relationships never reach their God-given potential. Alternatively, we can admit to our fears, coming out to face them, and in this way disarming them. As Paul Tournier says, 'The adventurous life is not one exempt from fear, but on the contrary, one that is lived in the full knowledge of fears of all kinds; one in which we go forward in spite of our fears.

3: The Adventurous Life

'If I should tell you how I really feel, would you still love me? If I should open the door to my secret self and let you look inside, would you be shocked, or worse still, would you laugh? . . . If I open myself to you like this I take a risk. A risk that you could use this knowledge to hurt, to humiliate and so to destroy our love. But with the risk there comes a possibility. The possibility that such knowledge could bind us together because our love is built on trust and understanding and reality.' (The Gift of Love*.)

I peered into the mirror of the hospital bathroom, shuddered and looked again. I barely recognised myself. It was hard to believe that this apparition with a face like a football had merely lost four impacted wisdom teeth — I looked as if I had been in a head-on collision with a double decker bus! And it was nearly visiting time. If my love saw me like this it would be the end of a beautiful romance for sure. I looked at my watch. It was too late to phone and say that

I was too ill for visitors. There was only one thing for it. I did what I could to improve things (without much success!) and made a dive for my bed. I would have to keep the covers up over my face and hope that he wouldn't notice how much further than usual I had fallen from being one of the 'beautiful people'. I pulled the sheet up over my nose, harem-style, and waited — but there was no escape. Two minutes before the visitors streamed into the ward, my doctor arrived to examine his handiwork and when Gordon reached my bed-side, there I was, battered, bruised and trapped right out in the open for all the world to see.

Our relationship was never quite the same again — but the change was definitely for the better. That night, one mask at least was laid aside, and we took a vital step from romance to reality. Even so, in spite of the fact that he had seen me at my worst, physically, it was some months before I plucked up the courage to confess to Gordon how I had *felt* about him seeing me, and how my plans to protect myself had been frustrated. It would seem as if baring oneself physically (especially when it is only to a fairly limited degree!) is less painful than mental and emotional nakedness. If you think that this is a very sweeping statement ask yourself this question: Which would I fear most, and find most damaging to the way I feel about myself? —

To be seen looking my least attractive physically by those whose love and acceptance is most important to me?

or

to open my heart to them and then find that as a result I might be:

laughed at

criticised

judged or condemned

misunderstood

giving someone a weapon that he or she might use against me in the future

laying myself open to unwelcome or threatening advice

showing more emotion than I would choose to

getting too involved

causing conflict
upsetting the status quo — possibly destroying the degree of
closeness that I have achieved with you by attempting to
improve it.

Perhaps you have never really stopped to analyse why
you react as you do; why you are reluctant to let your inner
self be known or why you take certain steps to keep others
at arm's length. But if we give a moment's thought I think
that most of us will agree that some, if not all, of these fears
have had us in their icy grip at some point in our lives, and
have limited our freedom to be ourselves and to get close
to others. This is true even though each fear has a positive
side and used in the right way, can be constructive and
helpful.

Take laughter for instance. Laughter can express many
things. It can be seen as a sign of happiness, a release from
tension or shared enjoyment. It can also imply different
things to people within the same situation, and, while expressing my genuine amusement, it can, at the same time,
appear to be a lethal weapon to you, wounding as effectively
as any tempered steel. This happened in our family not
long ago.

The squeaks and shrieks coming from the recorder
sounded like a cross between the bagpipes and a soul in
torment. Eventually the dog could bear it no longer. He
lifted up his nose and howled dismally, reducing the rest
of the family audience to helpless mirth.

'Don't laugh — it's not funny!' yelled the small musi-
cian, bursting into tears and hurling the offending instrument across the room. It was useless to try and assure her
that it was the dog who had provoked our laughter. She
refused to be comforted. We had laughed and that was
enough. It was a very long time before she could be persuaded to play to us again.

Children do hate to be laughed at, but they are certainly
not the only ones. An ability to laugh at ourselves comes
slowly to most of us and never to some. And so we keep
those little weaknesses, the impossible, impractical dreams,

and the illogical fears well hidden — for fear of appearing foolish.

Another childhood fear that often stays part of us for life is a reluctance to be thought the odd one out; to be criticised for being different or failing to measure up to the expectations of others. When that person is someone whose good opinion is very precious to us, we are even more wary of saying things that could be misinterpreted, or admitting to faults or problems that might make them think less of us. All this is perfectly understandable but an awful pity, for these are often the very insights that bond two people together in a way that total perfection (if there ever was such a thing) could never do.

Bob and Joanne discovered that. 'When I first met her, Joanne seemed so good at everything she did and so well-organised that she didn't seem to need anything or anybody,' said Bob. 'She appeared to be so special that she was unreal. But when I discovered that she was afraid of driving on the motorways, was tone-deaf and had awful trouble keeping her accounts straight, I stopped simply admiring her and started to love her. We both came to realise that perfection on a pedestal is for plaster saints, not people, and that we had to be real with each other. From then on our relationship burst into life.'

Fortunate Bob and Joanne. They have reached that vital point in personal maturity where they can see and accept themselves and others as they are; people with faults and failings as well as gifts and graces. In doing so they have discovered part of the antidote to fear in their relationships. We shall be thinking about this in more detail a little later on, but for the moment let's realise one thing. If we allow ourselves to be persuaded that the advertising media's image of 'beautiful people' leading immaculate lives is reality, we are being taken in by the confidence trick of the century. Certainly we all want to be happy and to achieve the very best that we can in our lives and relationships, but we have to face the fact that if we demand perfection, either of ourselves or of others, we are sure to be disappointed.

Of course, it isn't easy to admit to ourselves, let alone to another person that we are less than perfect. It can be painful to acknowledge reality; and yet painful experiences and emotions are not necessarily something to be avoided at all costs for they can teach us a great deal about ourselves and our partners as Grace and Peter found out.

When I first met her Grace was a very troubled lady. 'I'll never confide in him again,' she said bitterly. 'In a rash moment I told Peter that, before I met him, I had fallen in love with John, my boss, who had a very unhappy marriage. We got on so well that our working relationship could so easily have developed into something deeper. John wanted it too and I was very tempted. But I knew that I couldn't stand before God and admit that I had been responsible, even in part, for the final break-up of someone else's marriage, and so I left the job and the country. One day I told Peter, and now, every time we have a row, that old relationship gets dragged up. And it seems so unfair because this experience has been a positive one if only because it has made me acutely aware of how much time and effort is needed to build a good marriage. So in that way our relationship has benefitted. But in other ways my sharing has almost ruined things. I just wish that Peter could see that this has been one very small part of my life, which has made me what I am now, just as much as anything else that happened before. I will never be able to tell him any other personal things after this. It would be like locking an urban guerilla into an ammunition factory!'

A few weeks ago, a very different person was drinking coffee with a group of friends; one from whom all bitterness had gone. Grace told us that she and her husband had gone to a counsellor for help and had both found that they had a great deal of sorting out to do. Peter had been brought to realise that it was not what he had considered to be 'Grace's weakness' that was threatening their marriage, but his own jealousy, fear and lack of acceptance. And Grace had discovered why Peter had felt so threatened by her disclosure, and that there is a right and wrong moment for every revelation.

'I think that it's been worth all the difficulties,' she said with a wry smile, 'although at times I really wondered. We understand each other now better than we have ever done — and we're both beginning to talk more freely about how we feel, although I shall be more careful about how and when and what I say in future. I see now that people can only cope with so much that is difficult to accept, and, like the Bible says, there's a time to speak and a time to keep quiet!'

Helen, who had been very anxious about Grace and Peter's problems, shuddered. 'I don't think that all heart to heart communication is worth the risk,' she said. 'It came out all right for you on this occasion, but it might not have done. Why risk rocking the boat when you might end with something worse than you have already. I'd rather play it safe. You may not get so many "highs" but you won't get so many dreadful "lows" either.'

'Well, I think that the good is the enemy of the best,' said Claire firmly. 'It's easy to be satisfied with the bare minimum. It may be more comfortable to settle down into a rut, but I read somewhere that a rut is really a coffin, open at both ends, and I'm not ready for a coffin yet. I don't want to die without having really lived.' Fighting talk! Helen was right in a way, of course. It is a risky business to be real and open and honest. And many people do choose the safe option. But those of us who truly want to be free from fear and to see our relationships develop their full potential have to be willing to take that risk. We have to ask ourselves, 'do I want this so much that I am prepared to —

be honest when I would rather cover things up?

talk when I would rather withdraw into silence?

take responsibility for my actions when I would rather blame someone else?

stop and face the problem when I would rather run away?

admit that I don't know all the answers when I would prefer to appear certain and in control of the situation?

face the fact that we don't agree and be prepared to hammer things out, when part of me would choose peace at any price?'

That is quite a daunting list, isn't it? Does it seem like something that you couldn't possibly face? Take comfort in the fact that trust and understanding are like any other plants, they grow slowly. But before they can grow at all, they have to be planted. Many of us hesitate on the shores of Lake Communication and ask ourselves nervously, 'Can I trust him? (Or her?) Will he or she understand what I am trying to say? And like the little girl who said that she wasn't getting into the water until she had learned to swim — seemingly unaware of the fact that the only way to learn to swim was to get into the water — we ignore the fact that the only way to learn trust and understanding is to take the plunge and to start doing it. It is really an act of the will rather than the emotions, as we say to the one we love, 'I am going to trust you. I can't be sure that you will understand. Perhaps you will disappoint me or I you. But because I love you I am going to give you this very precious gift — my trust.'

4: Knowing Me

'It is a great grace of God to practise self-examination but too much is as bad as too little.' TERESA OF AVILA

Who am I?

'How would you rate my reasoning ability?' queried my eldest-born, glancing up from the book that he had been studying intently for the previous ten minutes. 'And what about original thought? Would you say that I was observant and original?'

'Why?' I asked cautiously, having learned long ago that home-truths aren't always well-received even when invited.

'Well, according to the bloke who wrote this book, I

need to sort out which of these personal qualities I've got, as a first step to deciding which careers I'd be best suited for,' said David, waving the relevant page in my direction. 'But I don't think that I know half the answers. This business of knowing yourself isn't as simple as it sounds, although he seems to be saying that it's the key to everything.'

I knew exactly how David felt. It *is* hard to stand back and see ourselves clearly and objectively and some of us, rather scared of what we may or may not find, hesitate to try. But although self-knowledge may be hard to come by, it is, as the Greek philosopher Socrates put it, 'the beginning of wisdom'. Which is, I imagine, why the type of multi-choice quizzes, which are supposed to offer you an insight into whether you are 'The Hostess-with-the-Most . . .!' 'A-Woman-that-Men-Hurry-Home-to' or 'The-Girl-Who-Will-Get-Ahead' (to name but a few) prove irresistible to nearly all of us!

For it isn't just the teenager in search of 'The Meaning of Life', a suitable career or a dream lover who needs to ask 'Who am I? Why am I here? Where am I going and how am I doing?' We all need to have an answer to these questions and the way that we answer them and the way that we feel about ourselves as a result, has an enormous influence on our minds, our behaviour and our relationships with others. If we look at ourselves and despise what we see, then the chances are that others will react towards us in the same way. As the cartoon character Charlie Brown put it:

'I'm always thinking of that little red-headed girl, but she doesn't think about me because I'm a nothing. And nobody thinks about a nothing.'

And, of course, the reverse is also true — if we are confident and happy, people tend to respond positively to us.

So you can see (in case you were wondering) this does have a very real bearing on the way we communicate with each other, and is the basic remedy for fear in our relationships. If I have faced the best and the worst in myself, and, all importantly, have come to God for forgiveness for where I have been wrong, strength to change what can be changed, help to accept what cannot be changed and the wisdom to know the one from the other, I can meet you and the whole world without fear.

But is it really a 'Good Thing'?

'I'm not sure that all this thinking about yourself is very healthy,' demurred one young mum, when we were discussing how we could understand ourselves better. 'And anyway I haven't got the time.'

Perhaps you feel like that too. If so, don't worry! I'm not suggesting that we should be permanently inward-looking, but that we should take stock, face facts and move on from there. And that is certainly more healthy than feeling depressed, purposeless and inadequate — which is what an enormous number of women complain of today. As for finding time, let's face it, we can always find time to do what is really important. So grab a quiet hour on your own (whether it means going to the library, sliding out of bed in the wee small hours, or locking yourself in the bathroom!) and let's see how you can discover what is going on in one very special and important part of God's creation — you!

Write it down

Even if you were hopeless at English at school and all you ever write today is a shopping list, it is a help to write down the answers to the questions at the end of the chapter. Having to put thoughts into written words concentrates the mind wonderfully, and stops you from thinking about what to have for dinner or how much the gas bill is likely to be!

Be honest

It is also important to be absolutely honest — remember no one is going to read what you have written except you, and it is a waste of time to try to fool yourself. You can always have a ceremonial bonfire afterwards if you feel anxious abut security! When you have written down your answers take a second look and ask yourself 'is that how I really feel, or is it how I think I ought to feel?' You may find that you have quite a few alterations to make. Sometimes we feel more comfortable and less threatened with half truths, especially in relation to ourselves, but it will only give us a distorted picture. Jesus said, 'You will know the truth, and the truth will set you free' (Jn 8.32). We need to consider three main areas of our lives: what we have done in the past, what we are doing in the present, and what we hope to do in the future.

Where have I been?

The past does have a bearing on the present. The person I am today has to a large extent been shaped by the pressures, pains and privileges of the years that have gone before. So if you want to understand where you're at, and why, give time to that first section, and don't dismiss it because it is water under the bridge.

Where am I now?

Have you noticed how life seems to creep up on you? If you're not very careful, it is easy to try to live as if your circumstances are the same as they were two or three years ago. But times change and we need to change and adapt to each new situation. For instance, at one stage in my life I had three under-fives whose grandparents lived a long distance from me. Now I have 5 school-agers and my parents and mother-in-law are retired and living just around the corner. Next year our eldest child may well be off to university and so the home situation and the demands it makes on me will change again.

We are often tempted to live in the future or the past, but we need to realise that *this* day is all the time that we can be sure of, and to take care that today is lived to the full. It is very easy to get the feeling, in today's youth-orientated culture, that once you are over 30, life deteriorates rapidly. Well, it need not? In fact, as we mature, life should be like cheese, and get more and more tasty! I love the white haired lady who declared roundly, 'This year I am 60, and I have no wish to be either older or younger. God planned that Jean Raddon would be 60 in 1982. Therefore, I am this age, at this time, in my present situation for his good purpose!' What a difference such an attitude makes!

What are my strengths?

I was hunting for some of my children and their friends among fifteen thousand other people at the Greenbelt Festival last year, when I was stopped in my tracks by two enormous badges pinned to the back of a tousled teenager strolling along ahead of me. One firmly proclaimed, 'God don't make junk', and the other implored 'Be patient; God hasn't finished with me yet'.

Some of us are very reluctant to admit to having any strengths. We are so pre-occupied with cultivating humility that we deny the gifts that God has given us. That is what is known as having a 'negative self-image' and is really an insult to our Creator. 'God don't make junk!'

My small daughter has a favourite tee-shirt. It is not particularly pretty. In fact it is a rather strange shade of blue and is now distinctly on the small side, but she still insists on wearing it. The source of its popularity lies not in its colour or its comfort, but in two words emblazoned across the front in swirling black letters which proclaim to the world that she is 'SOMEONE SPECIAL'. Even at 5 years old she knows what that means and she likes it! And if that is true for one little girl, it is equally true for each one of us. Charlie Brown has got it all wrong — there isn't one person who is a NOTHING! How could there be when every human being is SOMEONE SPECIAL to God?

Now don't misunderstand me! I'm not suggesting that we are all naturally good, and that we only need a little bit more education or better housing or wiser government or any other positive influence in order to reach our full potential. I agree absolutely with the apostle Paul when he says, 'all have sinned; all come short of God's glorious ideal' (Rom 3.23 LB). I have to agree with him; I know myself! But I know too from personal experience that what Paul

36

goes on to say is also true. 'God declares us "not guilty" of offending him if we trust in Jesus Christ, who in his kindness freely takes away our sins.' So if God forgives and accepts us just as we are, and equips us for the life he wants us to lead with both natural and spiritual gifts, who are we to say that he has not?

We have no need to cultivate a negative self-image, but on the other hand we have to beware of becoming proud, complacent and having the kind of self-love that the Laodicean church had. They saw themselves as having 'arrived' with material riches, status and power; in their own eyes they were a big success. But in God's eyes they were spiritually wretched, poor, blind and naked. What we *do* need is to see ourselves as we really are — in other words to have an accurate 'self-image', recognising that —

1. God created each one of us, just as we are, for a particular purpose (Ps. 139.13–16).
2. He loves us unconditionally and considers us to be so valuable that we are worth the death of his dear Son (1 Pet. 1.18–19).
3. If we have acknowledged our need and accepted the love and forgiveness that he offers, we have started a whole new life, adopted into God's family (2 Cor. 5.17).

Grasp those facts and never let them go, for it is this view of ourselves that brings peace of mind and enables us to love and relate to others.

'But even if I see myself in the right perspective', said Heather, 'I don't seem to recognise my gifts. What am I looking for anyway?

Natural abilities or the spiritual gifts that God gives?'

The simple answer is *both*, since both natural and spiritual gifts come from the same source. Of course, it isn't always easy to recognise them, but it can be done. The natural ones are more straightforward — after all, most of us know whether we can draw, sing, add up or have inborn talents in other directions. But we tend to think of spiritual gifts as being more difficult to define until we look at a list like the one in Romans 12.6–16. Then we are surprised at how down to earth they are. Check it out for yourself and see. The important thing is to be realistic about what you can't do as well as what you can, and to avoid trying to model yourself on someone else whom God has designed quite differently. Sometimes other people can give very helpful advice, but weigh their opinions carefully, or you may find yourself as a square peg in a round hole — it could have happened to me!

When David was about eight, he informed me in hushed tones that his friend's mother had just returned to work.

'Would you like it if I went out to work?' I asked, feeling that perhaps I was a below-standard mother in his eyes because of my 'stay-at-home' status.

'Well,' he said thoughtfully, 'I wouldn't mind if you were a secret agent.'

'What makes you think that I'd be any good at that?' I asked, wondering what previously undetected gift this small talent scout had spotted. 'You can run fast and you're good at making up stories,' he said, looking me over with narrowed eyes, 'and you look so ordinary that no one would guess!'

Needless to say, I didn't apply to Scotland Yard!

What are my weaknesses?

God loves and accepts us as we are but when we become Christians he doesn't wave a magic wand over us and make us instantly perfect — more's the pity! So in our thinking about ourselves (and other people) we need to remember the message on that other badge, 'Be patient; God hasn't finished with me yet.'

Everyone has weaknesses, problems and limitations; that is part of being human. The thing that will make a difference in our lives and in our relationships is not what the problems are, but how we react to them.

Take Jane, for example. When she was born, her parents wanted a son, and when her younger brother John came along six years later, all their interest and attention was poured out on the newcomer. During their childhood John was the one whose education took priority, who was encouraged to develop all his talents and interests, and for whom no expense was spared. Not unnaturally, Jane noticed and grew up feeling very much a second class citizen with little love for the rest of her family.

When she met Richard and fell in love with him, she saw marriage as an opportunity to escape and begin a new life. What she didn't recognise was that a change of name and change of address didn't automatically mean a change of person. She went into this new relationship carrying all the insecurities and resentments from the past with her, and as a result, the new life nearly ended before it was more than a few months old. It was only when she really grasped the fact of God's unconditional acceptance and unshakeable love for her that she dared to accept and love herself, which in turn allowed her to trust in, and respond to, Richard's love. It took a long time for all of the wounds of the past to heal, and Jane had to reach the point of being willing to forgive her parents for their neglect and to admit that her resentment and bitterness was also wrong and destructive to her, before she was really free.

You probably won't have the extreme problems that Jane had; most of us are more fortunate than that. But we all have dark areas in our lives that we need to face realistically. It is true that others are *in part* responsible for making us the way we are. But as adults we have a choice. We can choose to stay the way we are, bound by the past and allowing our problems to imprison us, or with God's help, we can accept the responsibility for ourselves in the present and see the problems as stepping-stones to growth and a new understanding of ourselves and others. Remember this. *We cannot fulfil the potential of today unless we live in the enjoyment of the present, free from the shadow of the past.*

Where am I going?

In her book *Total Joy**, Marabel Morgan says that we have two great needs — to be accepted and then directed. We need to have a purpose in life and a plan to get there. The Bible says, 'Where there is no vision, the people perish . . .' (Prov. 29.18). It also says, 'You saw me before I was born. The days allotted to me had all been recorded in your book, before any of them ever began' (Ps. 139:16,

GN). What a thought! God has a perfect plan for me and for you — and the most important thing that we can do is to find out what that plan is and work it out day by day with him. The questions are intended to give you a framework onto which you can superimpose that special plan — try them and see.

Knowing Me

WHERE HAVE I BEEN?

a) Who or what have been the most important influences in my life so far?
b) What 3 negative things from the past have contributed to making me what I am today?
c) What 3 positive things from the past have contributed to making me what I am today?
d) What have I accomplished?
e) Where have I failed?

WHERE AM I NOW?

a) What are my present relationships and commitments and how do I feel about them?

	Essential today	Optional today	Doesn't apply today	Happy with the way I'm coping	Unhappy with the way I'm coping	Neutral
People						
Marriage or other close relationships						
Children						
Parents (or in-laws)						
Rest of my family						
Friends						
Myself						
Money & Time						
Financial commitment (mortgage, HP, rent etc.)						
Debts						
Budgeting & general time & money management						

	Essential today	Optional today	Doesn't apply today	Happy with the way I'm coping	Unhappy with the way I'm coping	Neutral
The rest of my life						
Work (paid)						
Work (voluntary)						
Social						
Church activities						
Spiritual growth						
Others						

b) What can I do to improve my performance with essential commitments? and in vital relationships?

c) If time is a problem (too much or too little of it) what can I do to cut out inessentials or add worthwhile activities?

What are my strengths?

a) What 3 things do I like most about myself (List more if you can)?

b) What 3 things do I do best?

c) What relationships or activities bring me the most enjoyment?

d) What qualifications or experience do I have that I could use to help other people? Am I using them? If not, why not?

e) Am I sure that I am part of God's family?

f) Have I thankfully accepted all these good things as God's gift to me?

What are my weaknesses?

a) What 3 things do I dislike most about myself?
Whom do I consider to be responsible for them?
Can I change them with God's help or must I accept them (a bad temper can be dealt with; large feet cannot)?

b) Am I holding on to grudges and resentments about past hurts?

c) What am I afraid of?

d) What are the 3 things I find hardest to do?
Is God asking me to do them at all, or am I trying to model myself on someone else?

If I must do them, how can I improve my performance?

e) What would I least like my family and friends to know about me? If I am responsible for it, what am I going to do about it?

If it is an accident of birth or other circumstances why am I worried?

WHERE AM I GOING?

What I would like to have accomplished by this time next year in —

a) my personal life — physical, mental, spiritual
b) with my husband, children, friends.
c) within the home
d) within my job/hobbies or other outside activities
e) other things

Be specific!

Now choose one thing from each section and decide what you will do this week to work towards it. For instance, if you have decided to

a) lose weight
b) communicate more with your husband
c) do all the little jobs that you have ignored for the past five years
d) learn to paint and
e) travel abroad

this week you might decide to

a) choose your diet and get the children to eat up all the chocolate biscuits
b) fix up a baby-sitter so that you can go out together — even if it is only for a walk!
c) clean the paintwork in the bathroom
d) buy some paints and
e) open a travel fund — if you only put 25¢ in the piggy bank.

Remember, a journey of a thousand miles begins with a single step. Don't be put off because you can't see the entire map. Take the first step that God has shown you and trust him to show you the rest in his good time.

5: Knowing You

'Never think that you know it all; there is always more to learn. The most difficult and yet the most essential task in any relationship is to remain open to the continual discovery of your partner as a growing and changing personality.'

'The communication equation consists of two equally important parts — know yourself and know the one to whom you want to communicate. One half is of little use to you without the other.'

So says one professional communicator, and it really does make sense, doesn't it? However well we may feel that we know ourselves, communication is a two-way street, and we are not going to make any real progress along it unless we make as much of an effort to understand and accept other people as we do ourselves. This is why advertising companies, radio and television networks spend hundreds of thousands of dollars finding out what their target audience likes and dislikes, what they are thinking about current issues and why.

Throughout this book we are thinking particularly of how better communication can improve marriage and family relationships, but remember that these self-same principles can be applied to getting along with your boss, your next door neighbour or flat-mate. Understand what makes them tick and you are half-way home.

So how well do you know the people with whom you try to communicate day by day? Does familiarity make it difficult to distinguish the wood from the trees — have you drifted into the dangerous assumption that you know them all too well? Or do you share a fellow feeling with the lady who explained her frustrations to psychiatrist Paul Tournier in these words: 'My husband is a mysterious island. I am forever circling around it but never finding a beach where I may land.'

If you are in the first situation, try to see a person through the eyes of others, or in a different context. Ask yourself, 'What is he or she like at work, at school, or perhaps at home?' If you don't know, see if you can catch a glimpse of them there. You'll find it an eye-opener! It gives our communication quotient a real boost if I visit my husband at his practice occasionally. Not only do I get a fresh insight into the pressures and the problems that he faces day by day, but I see an entirely different side to his character!

But if you feel that you are all at sea, like Paul Tournier's patient (and at this point we are thinking particularly of communicating with men, whether it be your husband or another!) you will find it helpful to ask yourself these questions —

1. Am I aware of the basic differences in the emotional make-up of men and women?
2. Am I aware of how my husband sees himself in relation to the past, the present and the future?
3. Can I see and accept the difference in our particular temperaments?
4. Am I aware of my husband as a constantly growing and expanding personality?

1. AM I AWARE OF BASIC DIFFERENCES IN THE EMOTIONAL MAKE-UP OF MEN AND WOMEN?

Well, are you? Of course, the ardent feminists would argue that there are no essential differences, and that any that there are, are due to conditioning and sexist attitudes, but although many of us would agree that conditioning does play a part, we would also say that there is still an innate difference in the way that men and women approach life and tackle its problems. Men tend to be strong on forward-planning, logic, reason and objectivity, whilst women have decided strengths in the areas of detail, emotion and sensitivity. Stop now, before you read any further, and think how accurate that is for you and your husband. Of course, there are exceptions to every rule, and this may be true for you, only to a greater or lesser degree. But each couple needs to understand these differences as far as they affect them, and respond to them accordingly. Otherwise what seems a major drama to one will be dismissed as a minor irritation to the other and communication breaks down.

Take Don and Sue for example. The other day, Don (who has a very responsible job in the world of high finance) was on the office phone for about an hour and a half, negotiating a very tricky business deal, involving over a million dollars. During the time he was busy, his wife Sue rang through to his secretary six times, and was getting more and more upset each time the secretary said that he couldn't be disturbed. Eventually Don was free to talk to her, and discovered that her urgent need was also in the realm of high finance — she wanted to know what he had done with the money to pay the milk bill (yes, this really happened!). How would your husband have reacted in that situation? How would you? Would there have been an explosion of irritation, or would a sympathetic acceptance of the fact that if something is important to one person, then the other must take it seriously, have kept the peace?

2. AM I AWARE OF HOW MY SPOUSE SEES HIMSELF IN
   RELATION TO THE PAST, THE PRESENT AND THE FUTURE?

Let's think about the questionnaire in the last chapter that you worked through in relation to yourself, and see if we can apply some of the questions to the man in your life. We have discovered the importance of the past in our lives — what do you know about your husband's childhood? Not just the obvious things like where he lived and went to school, but what type of child was he, and what kind of relationship did he have with his parents and brothers and sisters. Most people love to reminisce, but if you feel that you can't ask your husband direct questions, you can often gather a great deal from casual family conversations. Most mothers love to talk about their children, so keep both ears open when your mother-in-law talks about hers!

Then there are his commitments in the present. What are his interests and what does he dread having to tackle?

45

What does he worry about? In one marriage survey the majority of men ranked money (or the lack of it!) as *the* major stress factor in their marriage, whereas their wives rated it as number 5. I wonder how many of those wives knew how their husbands felt, before the survey was carried out? How does your husband feel about his job, and the pressures on him in today's world where employment is often no longer secure?

'It's terribly hard for my wife to understand,' said one successful business executive. 'I seem to be doing quite well, but in fact there is such a pressure on me to produce more in terms of results that I seem to be running faster and faster just to stand still. The strain is enormous but she can't accept that success is as exhausting as failure and the line between them, today, is very thin.'

We shall be looking at planning for the future a little further on in the book, but there is one other thing we need to think about in this section. You probably know what you consider to be your husband's strengths and weaknesses, but do you know how he sees himself? It may be very differently. And what are you going to do about those character traits that annoy you?

You see it isn't enough to simply know another person in order to establish good communication — that only turns the lock half-way. The extra key that is needed to swing it wide open is what we do with the knowledge that we have, and how we react to the problems we find.

It is totally unrealistic to expect perfection — after all if I am not perfect, what right have I to demand perfection from others?

As Edith Schaeffer says in her book *What is a Family?** 'When people insist on perfection or nothing they get nothing!' Admittedly sometimes the difficulties loom so large that they distort our vision but even so they can be dealt with, if we are willing.

First of all, face up to those things that irritate you in your partner. Ask yourself, 'Am I willing to love him, not just for his good qualities, but for his problems? How many of these problems arise because I am not meeting his needs in certain areas?' Now consider what would happen to your relationship if you spent one hour a day dwelling on those negative things. Accept the fact that you cannot change anyone; pray about each fault individually, and ask God to bring about a change if that is necessary. Then tear the list up!

Now make a list of the positive qualities that attracted you to your husband in the first place (and all the others that you've discovered since!). Concentrate on one each day for a week — or longer if you've got a good long list —and look for opportunities to show your appreciation of these strengths. He may be a bit taken aback if you have previously been given more to criticism than compliments but persevere. Honest appreciation and admiration are great bridge builders and bridges are essential in a communications system.

3. CAN I SEE AND ACCEPT THE DIFFERENCES IN OUR TEMPERAMENTS?

Have you noticed how many people seem to choose a close friend or marriage partner who is very different to them in temperament? In some cases it appears as if they are complete opposites — she is quiet and retiring, and hardly opens her mouth in a group, while he is the life and soul of any social or business gathering. Or it may be the other way round. There are many bubbly extrovert chatterboxes who fall in love with strong and silent males — and after a short spell of marriage complain because their husbands have little to say. Oddly enough, some of these people seem quite unaware of how different they are! How about you? Have you got a realistic idea of how your temperaments match up? Do your differences act as a stimulus or a barrier to good communication?

With Christy and James the differences were not immediately obvious, but still very definitely there. You see, although they were both doctors and had other interests in common, the kind of life-style that they expected and accepted as normal was diametrically opposed. Christy had moved, not just from town to town, but from country to country as a child, and change, variety and the unexpected were the breath of life to her. James, on the other hand, was born and brought up in one place. He was a man of routine, and was happiest when life was peaceful and followed a fairly predictable pattern.

It is hardly surprising that they had plenty of problems in the first months of their marriage, but, although they were dismayed, they refused to be daunted. They were both determined to make a success of their marriage and so they tackled their temperamental difficulties in four ways; ways that are open to us all.

a) They talked things over. At this point their backgrounds were a help to them. After years of taking patients' histories they were both quite good at asking the right questions and sorting out the wheat from the chaff in the answers!

b) They were prepared to compromise. At first both Christy and James clung grimly to their own point of view, until they realised that there were benefits and draw-backs in both approaches to life. They acknowledged that the other's viewpoint was not better or worse, but just different, and they were able to pick out what was helpful to their lifestyle, abandon what was unhelpful and so create their own unique pattern.

c) They accepted what could not be changed. Most unhappy relationships are created by trying to change what cannot be changed. Christy and James recognised that they were not going to change the past or the basic temperament with which they had been born. So they made a positive effort to accept their individual differences, but to move as close together as they could within those limits.

d) They looked for the benefits of their situation. Although at times James found Christy exhausting and Christy found James unbearably staid, they recognised that he provided her with stability and security while she added sparkle and variety to their life together. So they regarded their differences as a bonus rather than a blight — for most of the time!

4. AM I AWARE OF MY SPOUSE AS A CONSTANTLY GROWING AND EXPANDING PERSONALITY?

How do you picture marriage? Do you regard the wedding as the ultimate destination rather than the beginning of a journey? Or do you see it as the first stage in a process of discovery, both individually and as husband and wife? If you answered 'yes' to the first you could be heading for problems. You see, the fact is that people do change and if you look at life as development in seven year spans (as some psychiatrists do) *that* is ten changes in a life-time of three score years and ten — six or more after you are married (assuming that you tie the knot somewhere between the ages of twenty-one and twenty-eight!).

If you accept that these changes take place, it is natural to assume that, if you are roughly the same age as your husband, you are also likely to be at the same stage of personal development. But, interestingly enough, this is not always the case. In her fascinating book, *Passages** the American writer Gail Sheehy says, 'During the twenties, when a man gains confidence by leaps and bounds, a married woman is usually losing the superior assurance that she once had as an adolescent. When a man passes thirty and wants to settle down, a woman is often becoming restless. And just at the point, around forty, when a man feels himself to be standing on a precipice, his strength, power, dreams and illusions slipping away beneath him, his wife is likely to be brimming with ambition to climb her own mountain.' Does that tally with your own experience? Can you trace a pattern of change in yourself and in your husband since your marriage? That has certainly been our experience. How do you react to the thought that the man you married two, five, ten or more years ago *is* a different person in some ways today?

Some people get very anxious at the thought of anything new happening in their own lives; others (like Ian in chapter 3) fear change in those they love because they are unwilling to change either their own ways or their opinions. But change can be an exciting challenge rather than a threat if —

1. We are aware that it will certainly come.
2. Accept it when it does.
3. Take positive steps to ensure that, even if we are developing at different rates, we are aiming to grow together and in the same direction.
4. Make sure that the image we have of each other is accurate and up-to-date.

These are not once in a life-time discoveries but an ongoing process, and I hope that by now you have a clearer picture of how to assess your progress so far.

So, having armed ourselves with some background knowledge of how communication works, gained some insight into our own needs and those to whom we want the message to get across, let's get to the nub of the whole business — and see how we can actually do it, in practical, everyday terms!

6: Building Bridges

'Behold the turtle; he makes progress only when he sticks his neck out!' JAMES BRYANT CONANT

Every human being longs to be loved and understood and these two very great and basic needs walk hand in hand. In fact, it is sometimes difficult to sort out the one from the other. If you understand someone it is much easier to love him; if you love him, you really want to understand. And the vital link between the two is effective communication.

Now, we have already noted that we communicate with all kinds of people for all sorts of reasons, in various ways and on many different levels. In order to do this we need time, sensitivity, insight and the ability to listen and express

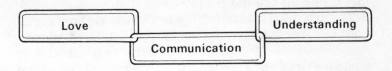

ourselves clearly. Most important of all, we need to be willing to start doing it. It is very easy (and very tempting!) to be like the tortoise or the turtle, and stay tucked inside our safe familiar shell while we think things over. But the turtle has to stick his neck out and become vulnerable in order to make progress and so do we. Which means that courage and willingness to take risks are vital. It is very easy to avoid a close encounter with another person, isn't it, by making excuses? If I suspect that my husband has something on his mind that I don't want to talk about, it is amazing how many urgent jobs just *have* to be done. And if I start a conversation with 'I've been thinking,' or go round the house with a certain look on my face, Gordon has been known to find a list of important phone calls to make, or to take refuge in the garden or even in church business!

Some people avoid their partners' efforts to communicate by using their children or friends as buffers — they are simply never alone together for long enough for meaningful conversations to take place. Others put an end to any subject that becomes threatening by shouting or retiring into hurt silence — and some folk can keep that up for days!

We need to be realistic and patient: don't be disappointed if real heart-to-heart sharing doesn't happen straightaway. Barricades that have been months or years in the building don't crumble at a touch, and the discovery of the real person behind the mask is a very slow process.

So much for the negative side. Now let's be positive. What can you do to bridge that space between you, deepen your understanding and love for each other and to make your sharing such a pleasurable experience for you both, that neither of you wants to avoid it?

The first thing to establish is whether you are both speaking the same language — that isn't as silly as it sounds. Remember that 70% of our communication takes place without a word being spoken, either by means of our actions or by means of our senses and emotions. So even if, like the majority of couples, you have the same mother tongue, the way in which you may understand the unspoken forms of communication could be very different. You see, we all have one way of expressing ourselves, our needs and our emotions, which comes more naturally to us than other ways. Problems arise however, when *your* natural way of expressing how you feel is not the natural way that *he* would use.

Let's imagine that you want to tell your partner that you love him — something we all want to hear! You could express this in words, but you may naturally prefer to demonstrate your love by *doing* something for him, or you may set out to show your love by trying to understand his emotional needs. Now that sounds straightforward enough on the surface, doesn't it? But supposing, since you are a very sensitive and emotional sort of person, you 'hear' love expressed most easily through your feelings. On the other hand, your husband is a man of actions, and to him they speak louder than anything else. What is likely to happen?

Picture the scene. It's evening time, and you have prepared a special dinner, hurried the children into bed early, lit the candles and put soft music on the stereo. All is ready for a romantic interlude. But as your husband comes through the door, his first words are, 'did you make that phone call that I asked you to?' . . . and you have forgotten! Do you think that he will 'hear' your message of love in the candles and Chicken Maryland? Well, he might, but he would hear it a lot more clearly if you had done the thing that he asked you to do, because actions are his primary language.

Of course, there are many other ways in which the same misunderstanding could occur. The husband who works long and late because he equates love with material provision, while his wife would swop all her kitchen gadgets for a few spoken words of affection and understanding; the wife who offers her husband Cordon Bleu cookery instead of a cuddle . . . the examples could go on and on. It is clear from this that if you want to lay a firm foundation for your bridge building you will need to start by becoming fluent in the language that *he* understands best. That doesn't mean to say that you can never have an in-depth discussion if he would choose whiter-than-white shirts as a demonstration of your care, but it does mean that if you up-grade your laundry procedure (if that is a point at issue between you!) he is more likely to hear what you say when you do talk!

If, (like me, when I was first presented with the idea) you aren't quite sure which language either of you lean towards naturally, the questions that follow will give you a clue. If your spouse will answer them too, and you can compare your answers, so much the better.

1. For an evening out my first choice would be
    a) a party with new and interesting people to meet and stimulating conversation
    b) a concert or film followed by a candle-lit supper in a small restaurant
    c) ten-pin bowling or other sporting activity
   my husband/wife's first choice would be ....
2. If my child came rushing home to tell me that he had done well at school I would want to —
    a) discuss what had happened with him at great length
    b) give him a hug and/or kiss (depending on his tolerance)
    c) take him into town and buy him a gift
   my husband/wife would ....
3. If I am alone and feeling miserable and depressed would I be most likely to —
    a) phone up my friend/husband/wife
    b) climb into a hot bath with a radio to listen to and a book to read
    c) go out and dig the garden
   my husband/wife would ....

4. During childhood I knew that my parents loved me because they —
   a) told me so often
   b) spent time with me
   c) gave me most things that I wanted
my husband/wife knew because ....
5. When we have a disagreement I am most likely to —
   a) argue my point quietly but determinedly
   b) withdraw into silence
   c) march up and down the room or bang on the table
my husband/wife would ....
6. I wish my husband/wife would more frequently —
   a) discuss his/her interests with me
   b) be romantic and rash
   c) help me in practical ways

How to score: mostly a's — your primary language is words
mostly b's — your primary language is emotional
mostly c's — you are an Action woman!

Once we have got our 'language problems' sorted out, we will want to translate theory into practice, and for this we need time. Meaningful communication rarely just 'happens'; time must be found for it, and in the hectic lives that many of us lead, we are unlikely to find spare hours (or even minutes) just lying around — we have to carve them out of our programme deliberately.

A long time ago, Gordon and I discovered the joy and necessity of putting one evening a week on one side for a 'date' with ourselves. It hasn't always happened, but when our children were small, Sunday evening after church was usually a good time to compare our diaries, make plans for the week ahead and talk together. Then, nearly two years ago, our family expanded by two, very unexpectedly, and we found that adapting to and caring for a family of five children ranging in age from four to fifteen left us without a moment to think, let along communicate! There never seemed to be a job or child-free moment!

Eventually we decided that the only solution was to leave home! We couldn't afford to go out for a meal every week, and long walks on a winter's evening do more for the circulation than communication, so we simply swopped houses — in our case with my parents or mother-in-law, but it could equally well be done with friends. In somebody else's home there are no jobs that clamour for your attention; if the telephone rings it isn't for you, and as you relax, it becomes easier to think, plan and share together.

In some situations of course, it isn't possible to make a regular date, and you need to have an emergency procedure worked out. Claire's husband, for instance, is a university don, and Claire sees very little of him during term-time, but of course they do have the opportunities during the long vacations to catch up with each other. The trouble was though, that Claire used to find that problems and ideas would crop up during term-time which there was no opportunity to discuss at length, and by the time the 'vacs' came, she had lost the urge to talk about them, or she no longer had a clear picture in her mind of what they were. The result was frustration on her part and poor communication for them both. Now they have a new system. Claire keeps a page in her diary in which she jots down anything she wants to discuss with Patrick as and when it occurs. They have agreed that when the list reaches a certain length they will give top priority to making time to talk things through. They are ruthless about implementing this, and their communication rating has improved enormously as a result.

Even when they have time, many people need a catalyst to their communication and there are various ways of getting the pot simmering — other than sheer desperation!

Jenny found life was getting difficult when Bill took on leadership responsibilities within their church. Although they had both made the decision that it was right for him to do this, and Jenny had promised to support him, she found herself getting more and more irritated and tense because he was out so often, and until so late. But she felt guilty about complaining because this was a joint decision and spiritual work to boot! One night she could bear it no longer. Bill had promised to be home by 10.00 pm and when at 11.15 he still hadn't arrived, Jenny went to bed, locking both the front and the back door. When Bill couldn't get in, he thought at first that Jenny had simply locked the door by mistake. But when it took him a quarter of an hour to rouse her, he began to sense that something could be wrong! Jenny had sent up a distress signal by her action, which ensured that they had to talk about a problem which she felt unable to raise in the normal way.

Some couples find that talking a problem over with a third person present is very helpful. It doesn't seem to matter whether this person is a trained counsellor, or just a wise and sympathetic friend, who can help both parties express themselves clearly by asking the right kind of questions. And it doesn't have to be a formal interview.

Mary felt very resentful about the long hours worked by her minister husband, and yet she also felt guilty and unable to talk about it because it seemed un-Christian to resent his service to God and to so many needy people. One day she and her husband had a meal with friends who were in much the same situation except that, in their case, the husband was away from home a lot because he commuted to London and had frequent overseas business trips. As the two men discussed the pressures of their working lives, their wives were able to explain how *they* felt. The relief of knowing that others experience the same pressures and tensions, even if it was in a slightly different context, gave Mary a freedom to express herself that she had never had before, and the barriers, once lowered, were never raised so high again.

Another way of stimulating communication that many have found useful is to write down how they feel. Now before you dismiss the idea out of hand as hopeless for you, just think for a minute. A blank piece of paper doesn't get bored, it doesn't cry and it doesn't get angry. It allows you to finish what you want to say without interruption, and if you find that it is 'coming out all wrong' you can cross it out and start again without anyone having been hurt or irritated by your incoherence. In her book, *Two into One**
Joyce Huggett suggests that couples should each keep a notebook that they use only for this purpose, and they should set aside say half an hour to consider one particular problem. For the first ten minutes each individual writes

down how he or she feels about the matter in hand, concentrating on expressing feeling rather than criticism or blame. After ten minutes or so they exchange books and read very carefully what the other has written. Then — and this is the tricky bit — talk about what you have written, clarify any misunderstandings and decide how you will proceed in the light of what you now know about each other. It may sound a bit foolish and embarrassing but many couples have really found it a help, so why not give it a try with this question:

What are the three things that we have done or experienced together that have given me the most pleasure in our relationship so far? What are the three things that have given me the most pain? You won't lose anything by it and you could gain a great deal.

7: Language of Love

'Speech is God's gift. We shall have to account for it. It is through words that we communicate with each other and we reveal what we are. We haven't the right to be silent, but speaking is a serious matter, and we must weigh our words in the sight of God.' (MICHEL QUOIST, 'I spoke, Lord' in Prayers of Life*)

I don't think that the Russian author Dostoyievsky was feeling much in favour of non-verbal communication at the time when he wrote, 'much unhappiness has come into the world because of bewilderment and things left unsaid'. But I suppose that since he was an author, his primary language was likely to have been words, spoken and written! Be that as it may, there comes a time when, if bewilderment is to be avoided, even the shyest and most reserved amongst us has to venture into speech.

My friend Leonie recognised this when she said, 'we may do a great deal of our communicating without talking, but I think that this is mainly because many of us are so bad at expressing ourselves properly in words that we are afraid to try. Eventually though, we find that the talking has to start if we are ever going to understand each other fully.' And she is right, of course.

The trouble is that there are so many pitfalls for the unwary. As an ancient aunt inscribed in my childhood autograph book —

'It's not so much what we say to our friends,
As the manner in which we say it.
What would an egg amount to today
If the hen stood on the perch to lay it?'

I find that very picturesque! The Bible tells us that 'your speech should always be pleasant and interesting, and you should know how to give the right answer to everyone' (Col. 4.6, GNB) but so many of our attempts at talking things over end up like a perch-laid egg: an awful mess!

How can we put that right? At the beginning of the book we thought in some detail about how the communication works. In every conversation there is a transmitter (the person speaking) and a receiver (the person listening) and it is in these two areas of speaking and listening that we need to fine-tune our performance, if the message is to beat the filters and be received and understood as we intend it to be.

Let's look at speech first. There is a great deal that could be said about it, but for the sake of simplicity we will imagine that Eileen and Jerry have a problem about the way that he spends his spare time. Whilst Eileen can just about tell the difference between a flower and a weed, Jerry is an avid gardener and, at his insistence, their whole life-style revolves around the garden season. Jerry is very reluctant to go on holiday in the summer because that is just the time when his prize flowers and vegetables need his most careful attention; the children's ball games are frowned upon in case they damage the herbaceous borders or make holes in the lawn, and when Jerry is not disbudding, hoeing or staking up his plants, he is fully occupied with running the local Horticultural Society. There are times when Eileen feels that she would get more attention if she was a basket of tomatoes!

Now Eileen has spent a great deal of time and energy trying to solve the problem. She has tried to divert Jerry's interests into other channels and failed. On the principle of 'if you can't beat them you will have to join them' she has tried to share his enthusiasm, but it's not really her 'thing' and she just cannot enter into or appreciate his total absorption in this one thing, so a degree of tension remains. Jerry for his part is hurt that Eileen doesn't seem to appreciate the abundant supply of flowers that he cuts for the house, the quantities of fruit and vegetables he provides or the lovely surroundings he has created for their home. They have tried to discuss the whole issue but it has always ended in conflict. Is there anything else that Eileen can do? Yes, there is!

1. ACCEPTANCE

First of all Eileen has to convince Jerry that she loves and accepts him as a person. She has to show him, by her words and/or by her attitude that her love and acceptance is not conditional. He does not have to agree with her or share her feelings about the garden, in order for her to love him. In other words, she has to make a deliberate decision not to try and bludgeon him into accepting her point of view. After all, a man convinced against his will is of the same opinion still! This does not mean, of course, that she can never question his behaviour, but it does mean that when she does, it is his behaviour, and that alone, which is the point at issue. His worth as a person doesn't come into it.

Now Jerry's feeling of self-worth and acceptance by Eileen have taken a bit of a battering in the past, because by criticising anything so dear to his heart as his garden, it has seemed to Jerry that Eileen has been criticising him personally. So it is important that this is put right and when it is, Eileen may feel that he has a different attitude to her needs. We are often prepared to give freely what we will never permit anyone to take from us by argument or force.

2. SEEING THE REAL ISSUE

In a court of law, the facts are critically important. They are either right or wrong and a decision is made accordingly. But in our sharing together, especially within marraige, the *facts themselves* are not so much the basic issue as *how we feel* about them and how we respond to them. In preparing to talk about her problem Eileen has to consider four questions —

a) How do *I* feel about this problem?

b) Are *you* willing to respect my feelings?

c) How do *you* feel about this?

d) Am *I* willing to respect your feelings?

and all the time she has to keep one vital fact before her: 'my position is not better than yours; it is just different from it.'

3. OWNING THE PROBLEM

When we have a problem, we almost always see it in terms of being the other person's fault, don't we? We are very quick to criticise or blame, and the natural and immediate response is self-defence and counter attack! Which is the certain recipe for a full-blown row as Eileen and Jerry would tell you.

But supposing Eileen approached things from a different direction by accepting that the problem between them is not because of what Jerry is doing but because she can't cope with the feeling that something else has a more important place in Jerry's life than she does. By owning the problem as hers she can talk about it without appearing to attack Jerry and he is more likely to listen sympathetically. Hopefully he will come to see that his behaviour has a part to play in causing the problem, and accept the responsibility to change. But this can't be forced on him.

4. USING AN I MESSAGE

In order to 'own the problem' Eileen needs to use an 'I' message. An 'I' message has three parts. It pin-points an action or behaviour, an emotion, and the impact that the action or behaviour has on you. Eileen might express her problem to Jerry like this:

Behaviour ('When')	Emotion ('I feel')	Impact ('Because')
When I see so little of you in the summer	I feel miserable	because I want to share my interests with you sometimes.

'I' messages are not always down-beat, of course. We can talk about positive feelings that way, and it is always helpful to express appreciation before touching on negative feelings. In fact, I would go as far as to suggest that for every criticism there should be at least three complements, and it should *all* be said with love which corrects without condemning and counsels without demanding its own way. For instance, Eileen might preface her remarks by letting Jerry know how glad she is to have a freezer full of home-grown vegetables for the winter by saying —

Behaviour	Feeling	Impact
When you keep us so well supplied with vegetables	I feel so grateful	because it is a real help with keeping our food bills down.

She can also ask for his help with the problem and perhaps suggest alternatives which would make things better from her point of view. She might say —

Behaviour	Feeling	Impact
If you could help by taking an early holiday	I would feel happier	because I would know that we would have some uninterrupted time together.

There is one particular thing to remember about using 'I' messages. The 'I' message means that you are speaking for yourself; explaining your *own* thoughts, your *own* feelings and sensations and your own intentions. Stick to that. You are an authority on yourself: no one can know what is going on inside you unless *you* tell them. But don't fall into the trap of speaking for other people. 'My parents feel the same' or 'The children all want to do it'. That invites arguments, for you are an authority on your *own* feelings only.

You may feel that it is an unnatural way to express yourself and you couldn't do it. Well of course, we are bound to feel a little ill at ease with any new way of doing things at first, but practice makes perfect, and if you stop to ask yourself how you would react if approached in this way rather than with accusations and blame, I think you may feel that it is worth giving it a whirl! Using 'I' messages has got positive advantages over using 'You' messages (which we will consider next) because —

a) you take responsibility for the problem

b) you show honesty and openness

c) you share with your partner the effect his behaviour is having on you, which is less threatening to him than suggesting that he is intrinsically bad because he is doing certain things

d) you place a responsibility on your partner to be considerate of the needs and feelings of others

e) you show that you respect your partner and his needs but at the same time show that your needs are important too

f) you are dealing with actions and behaviour, not his self-esteem. You are not attacking his personality or his character. You have a right to question your partner's behaviour, but you have no right to question his worth as a person made in God's image

g) you demonstrate trust that your partner cares about your needs and is really ready to help you.

'You' messages

This is commonplace communication — probably because many of us have never thought of doing it any other way. A 'You' message conveys the idea that the speaker is the normal person, in the right and seeing the situation clearly, while the hearer is abnormal, defective and wrong. Sadly, 'You' messages are heard daily in every household throughout the land. Let's leave Eileen and Jerry and bring the example a little closer to home.

In our house we have a large collection of mugs and a large amount of tea and coffee is consumed during the day, particularly during the school holidays. Unfortunately, my children seem incapable of returning their mugs to the kitchen and washing them up when dirty; they simply help themselves to a clean one until the supply is used up — which is usually about 10.00 pm when Gordon or I want to make the bedtime drinks! You can imagine the scene that follows, and when 'You' messages like 'Why can you never remember to do what you're told? You're doing nothing all day and still you can't be bothered to wash up after yourselves' are used the day can end on a sour note. If, however, I can remember to phrase it in an 'I' message such as 'When you leave your mugs around, it makes me feel fed-up, because it seems as if you can't be bothered to do what I have asked you to' it is amazing what a difference it makes!

You may like to test out your understanding of 'I' and 'You' messages by thinking how you could have applied them to recent disputes in your household. If all has been sweetness and light recently and nothing comes to mind, try it out on the following —

1. Your child is very late home from school and you have had no message to warn you that this will happen. When she gets home you discover that she has been shopping with a friend and forgot to phone you.
2. Your husband has committed you to spend an evening with friends without consulting you, and you already have a prior engagement for that date.
3. Your sister/roommate/friend has made a joke about something you said or did which you feel made you look foolish in front of your friends.

8: Love that Cares, Listens

'Listen before you answer. If you don't you are being stupid and insulting.' (Prov. 18.13, GNB)
'God gave us two ears but only one mouth, which the Irish have interpreted as a divine indication that we should listen twice as much as we talk'
(JOHN POWELL, *The Secret of Staying in Love**)

If money was no object, what would you select as the best possible gift that you could give to someone you love? Day-dream for a moment. Would it be something in the material realm, costly and beautiful? Or would it be practical care, providing for all their physical needs? Believe it or not, many psychiatrists would advise you to think again if you chose anything from those areas, for according to them, one of the greatest gifts that we can give to anyone is to listen to them; not just to hear what they are saying but to listen to them with love.

Perhaps you are wondering where the distinction lies and whether there is any real difference between listening and hearing. There certainly is. The dictionary defines 'hearing' as 'to perceive with the ear' whereas listening is explained as 'to hear what is said *with attention*. To make *an effort* to hear'. When I am *hearing* you, my prime intention is to gain information for my own purposes. My awareness while I am hearing you is directed towards myself; I am thinking about how *I* am reacting to what you are saying and how *I* intend to respond. When I listen to you, on the other hand, my attention is focused on you; I am trying to understand how *you* see the situation and how *you* feel about it.

Sadly we hear each other far more often than we really listen. And what is more, it has been said that —

we hear only half of what is said to us

we understand only half of what we hear

we believe only half of what we understand

we remember only half of what we believe

If that is only half true(!) it is not surprising that the majority of conversations that take place fall into the category of 'non-communication' or 'dialogues of the deaf'.

Be a better listener

There are real skills involved in being a good listener — skills that anyone can learn, once we realise what they are.

1. WATCH YOUR ATTITUDE

The way in which you feel about the person to whom you are listening will colour what you hear. If you find him boring, irritating or tiresome this attitude will filter out part of his message. In addition, he will probably sense your lack of sympathy and will be unable to communicate so freely. Which brings us back once more to the vital needs of acceptance one by the other.

2. DONT SWITCH ON THE AUTO-PILOT

Did you know that you can listen or receive spoken messages five times as fast as you can speak? Which means that if you partner is speaking at the rate of one hundred words per minute and you are capable of hearing five hundreds words per minute, there is quite a bit of extra time to fill. If your husband is the slow and reflective kind of conversationalist, or you have heard his story twenty times before, there is a strong temptation to nod off or to switch onto auto-pilot! Mothers of pre-schoolers will recognise a particular temptation in this direction, but problems arise when you employ the same technique with another adult! Your three year old may not notice your pre-occupation, but your husband certainly will!

3. WATCH OUT FOR SELECTIVE LISTENING

Experts in communication science tell us that we read and listen selectively. In other words, there is a strong tendency to filter out anything that we don't want to hear or that we disagree with. We've all had the experience of the 'I told you that' — 'No, you didn't' conversation. You may be genuinely convinced that your husband didn't tell you about his evening meeting, and yet in a large percentage of cases, a tape recording of the original conversation would reveal that he did tell you, but for some reason you didn't want to hear and simply filtered it out.

4. GIVE YOUR FULL ATTENTION

Have you ever tried talking to someone who is only giving you half their attention? You don't feel free to say very much, do you? Kate had a practical demonstration of this at a conference she attended recently. During a training session on expressing themselves clearly, the group was divided into two's, told to sit knee to knee and give each other their total attention while one of the partners spoke for one minute on a subject about which they felt strongly. When the minute was up, the procedure was reversed, the first speaker becoming the listener, but on this occasion the latter was instructed to be very inattentive, to fidget, shuffle, gaze all round the room, or appear to be bored to death. The feelings of the speakers were then compared. In the first instance, they agreed that they felt enabled to speak freely and were able to find real relief in expressing themselves to someone who was all attention. But on the second occasion even the most fluent talkers found that they were inhibited; some dried up completely; and others became angry and began to shout.

Kate went home excited by this discovery and poured it all out to Margaret, who had often complained that her husband had little to say. Margaret was downright sceptical. She didn't see how such an apparently minor thing as giving full attention to someone could make any real difference, but she decided to give it a try, just to prove to Kate that it wouldn't work for her. A few days later, Margaret was sitting reading when her husband came into the room, and made a casual comment about what he had just been doing in the garden. Margaret seized her chance. Instead of just glancing up from her book as she would usually have done, she put it down, swung her legs up onto the settee so that she was relaxed and comfortable, and gave her husband her full attention. To her amazement, he talked non-stop for the next hour!

5. LISTEN WITH YOUR HEART AS WELL AS YOUR EARS

Hearing is only one of our five senses, and even when someone is talking to you, there is as much to be gathered from the way the words are said, the posture and attitude of the speaker, as from the words themselves. In fact, there is more. Apparently, when we are speaking we express 7% of our meaning through the words we use; 38% of our meaning through the tone of our voice, and 55% of our meaning through our non-verbal behaviour — in other words, the way in which we stand, sit, look, smile, scowl, clench our fists, and a whole host of other things. So eyes are every bit as important as ears when we are listening. Touch too has a part to play. Your partner may assure you that al is well with his words, but if you put your arm around him and he is stiff and unyielding, he is giving you a mixed message — beware! If you are puzzled, you may pick up some helpful clues from the tone of his voice. A flat monotonous drone suggests depression; whiners may be trying to manipulate; a high-pitched squeak indicates excitement or agitation, and a brisk no-nonsense approach gives the impression of meaning what he says. The emphasis put on any given word in a sentence can change the meaning too. Try saying 'When you have finished, will you please clear the table' or some other simple request with a different word stressed each time, and ask your family for their reaction. It's quite an eye-opener!

6. BE A REFLECTIVE LISTENER

This does not mean that you doze off into a 'brown study' while your partner is talking, but that you reflect back to your partner what you heard, so that he can confirm that you understood him properly, or clarify the message if you have any misconceptions. This process is very important. Remember that the filters that we discussed earlier always distort the message to some degree, so you can only report back what you heard, which will never be identical to what he said. And as you use your eyes, your touch and your own sensitivity to try and understand the way he is feeling, and reflect it back, you can often help him to understand himself more clearly.

Imagine that you have a young family and when your husband comes in in the evening he is more likely to get a towel-wrapped toddler than a soothing cup of tea thrust into his arms. He might say to you, 'Sometimes I think that the Victorian fathers had a lot going for them.' Now, his tone of voice and the twinkle in his eye could signal that all is well. On the other hand, there could be a steely gleam and turned down mouth which could prompt you to reflect back, 'It sounds as if you think that they had a better deal than you do', to which he might reply, 'Well, they certainly weren't expected to play nursemaid after a hard day's work'. At this point you have to restrain yourself from pointing out all the domestic help that Victorian mothers had and reflect back, 'Are you saying that, you feel that I expect you to help too much in the evening?'

In reflective listening you are doing several things —

a) you are not trying to tell him how he should or should not feel. You accept that he does feel that way, rightly or wrongly

b) you show that you understand how he feels, even if you can't agree with those feelings

c) you don't defend yourself or attack him

d) when you don't quite understand what he is saying to you, you ask for clarification by using phrases like, 'am I hearing you correctly?', 'are you saying that . . .?', 'can you give me an example of what you mean?'

7. BE PATIENT

There is a great temptation, especially if you are going over an old problem, to think that you know all that he is likely to say, and to jump in with pre-conceived ideas, solutions or comments. But hear him out. Let him finish and listen as carefully on the tenth occasion as you did on the first. You may well hear or sense something new. When you have heard it all, and only then, you can respond with how you feel about the situation in an 'I' message, at which point he becomes the receiver.

Talking about a problem in this way may not suggest or bring about an immediate solution but at least the partners will both know exactly how the other one thinks and feels. And this is a major step forward. So often a problem can't be solved because they don't really know what it is. Once they do, and are more anxious to understand than to prove themselves right, it can be handled constructively.

And when you do discover a solution or agree upon a course of action, put it into words and spell it out aloud to one another. To say, 'Well, let's see then, we agree that we both felt . . . and we will tackle it by . . . and . . . and . . .', will clarify your decision and give you both a feeling that the thing is being dealt with and you know where you are going.

8. DO NOT RESPOND WITH

a) Instant answers

It's very easy to pronounce your pat solution with a 'If I were you . . .', 'In your position I would', 'The answer to that is . . .'. Stop! For the most part that is not what he is asking you for. He is asking to be heard and understood. If he wants practical help he will let you know.

b) Stop-gap solutions

You may want to bring the conversation to an end and so you say things like, 'It will work out', 'Don't worry', 'You'll soon feel better'. He doesn't want to be soothed so much as to know that you feel the hurt with him. To identify with one's partner in this way is to be Christ-like, for Jesus was 'touched with the feeling of our infirmities (Heb. 4.15, AV). He got right down to where we are, and we need to do the same for others.

c) Diagnoses

You may say 'You don't really mean that', 'What you need to do is . . .', 'What's wrong with you is . . .'. This isn't reflective listening. Your job at this point is to understand *what* he feels. *Why* he feels it is his to discover — you may be asked for your opinion or help. You may not. That is up to your partner.

9. RECOGNISE THAT THERE IS A RIGHT TIME AND PLACE FOR THIS DEEP LISTENING

Listening is hard work and most of us find that there are times when this degree of concentration and self-giving is almost impossible. If we are very tired or frustrated or pre-occupied with our own problems, all our available energy is used up in listening to ourselves! You know what it is like when you have both had a bad day. As your husband arrives home you are in no state to listen to tales of woe from his world until you have unloaded your aggravation about the children, the gas-man or your impossible boss. And he feels the same way. Which is where the old adage 'Never discuss a problem standing up or on an empty stomach' must come from. Choose the right time and place for heart to heart sharing and it will be of infinite benefit to you both. Choose the wrong time and you could end up with a first class fight. Which brings us to the form communication that most of us avoid like the plague — conflict!

9: Fight a Good Fight!

*'Discussions become quarrels when our words generate
more heat (emotion) than light (understanding).*
'Don't make too much of too little too often!'

If your friend tries to persuade you that she *never* gets into
conflict with her nearest and dearest, you can be sure of
one thing: she is either trying to deceive herself or to deceive
you! The plain truth is that every close relationship has its
difficulties and disagreements. It isn't the fact that we have
these problems, but the way in which we deal with them
that is crucial. Paul Tournier says, 'Those who make a
success of their marriage are those who tackle their problems together and overcome them. Those who lack the
courage to do this are the ones whose marriage is a failure'
(*Marriage Difficulties*★).

Since human life is so full of conflict it is hardly surprising that the Bible has a great deal to say about how we
should act and react towards one another. One of the key
passages is in Paul's letter to the Ephesians in which he
says,

'No more lying, then! Everyone must tell the truth . . . if you
become angry, do not let your anger lead you into sin, and do
not stay angry all day. Don't give the devil a chance . . . Do
not use harmful words but only helpful words, the kind that
build up and provide what is needed, so that what you say will
do good to those who hear you. And do not make God's Holy
Spirit sad; . . . Get rid of all bitterness, passion and anger. No
more shouting or insults, no more hateful feelings of any sort.
Instead be kind and tender-hearted to one another and forgive
one another as God has forgiven you through Christ' (Eph.
4.25–32, GNB.).

Did you notice as you read those words that Paul assumes
that there will be times when we will be angry and that that
in itself is not wrong? Anger is neutral; it is what we *do*

with that anger that is the vital issue. Very often as Christians we feel guilty about being angry and try to suppress it. When we do this, it is as if we push the anger down into a bottle and use our guilty feelings as a stopper to prevent the anger from bubbling out. But as Dr Marion Ashton has wisely pointed out, if when we bury these emotions, we bury them alive, they will eventually erupt, and do so with additional force, because they have been compressed and suppressed for so long. If this is the case then we obviously need to deal with our anger quickly. Many of us may have tried our own remedies or those of other people and found them only partly satisfactory, so let's see what the biblical answer to conflict is.

1. TELL THE TRUTH IN LOVE

We are very good at telling half-truths to ourselves and each other, aren't we? Couples seem to react in one of three ways when it comes to conflict in their relationship. The first reaction is to deny that it exists. This happens when a very strong personality dominates a weaker one to the extent that the quieter partner is never allowed to express an opinion or expected to form a judgement on anything. The second reaction is to avoid conflict at all costs. These couples go to great lengths to avoid any touchy subjects in their conversations together, and eventually their unresolved problems can turn their marriage into a quagmire — green and pleasant looking on the surface, and full of hidden nastiness underneath. The third group are more open. They admit that they have problems, and look for ways of resolving them. Unfortunately, even then we sometimes stumble into forms of communication that are less than honest, in our efforts to sort ourselves out.

a) *the Double Bind message* where we give two messages, one of which contradicts the other — we've all used that at times. You know the kind of thing. I am sitting slumped in the chair, quietly seething about something that has gone wrong, when my husband comes into the room and switches on the television for the International Soccer match. 'Do you mind if we watch the football?' he enquires. 'If you want to,' I reply through gritted teeth. A few minutes later he notices that I'm still gazing into space and tears his mind away from the game for long enough to enquire, 'Are you okay?' 'Yes, I'm just thinking,' I snarl provocatively. 'Oh, that's all right then,' he says thankfully (not reading my non-verbal signals at all) and turns his attention back to the battle on the football pitch, leaving me furious at his insensivity and fuming over the problem still.

b) *the Back Door message* is another popular form of half-truthful communication. You come back from a rare evening out with friends and you say sweetly and pointedly 'The Jones manage to have a meal out together most weeks', or your husband remarks, 'How does Jane find the time for all that Cordon Bleu cookery when she works full-time? Her organisation is amazing! Jim's a lucky man.' Both of you are hinting at some underlying irritation in your own relationship, but usually your partner ignores the hint, either by accident or design, and you are left more frustrated than before.

c) *then there is the Diversionary message*. This is a favourite one when you can sense a storm brewing that you want to avoid at all costs. The technique is that you launch into the attack first on another subject altogether, in order to avoid getting into an argument in which you feel you might be worsted, or into a situation you can't handle.

d) Another slightly dangerous communication game that some people play is the *Third Person* message. Eddie finds it very difficult to talk about his grievances to his wife Ruth. But they have close mutual friends in Matthew and Cynthia and when Eddie has a problem he tells Matthew, knowing that Matthew will tell Cynthia and Cynthia will tell Ruth. So eventually Ruth gets to hear about the difficulty, in what I should imagine must be a somewhat distorted form by the time it has passed through all those transmitters and receivers. Ann plays the game a slightly different way. She confides her problems to her mother-in-law, hoping that they will reach her husband Rob by this rather risky route. It is hardly surprising that in both these situations their communication problems aren't really resolving themselves.

2. DON'T LET YOUR ANGER LEAD YOU INTO SIN

Inevitably there will be things that happen in our day to day lives that makes us irritable or angry, but the anger and irritation become wrong when we nurse it to ourselves and let it fester. Paul tells us not to stay angry all day (or, in other biblical translations, not to let the sun go down while we are still angry) because in that way we give the devil a happy hunting ground.

Dr John Bettler, an American counsellor, says that we must outlaw 'gunny-sacks'. A gunny-sack is a large bag in which we store all the little grievances of the day, and many of us never move far without one! Let's take a peep into Sarah and Tom's house early in the morning. Tom has forgotten to set the alarm (his job) and so they oversleep and start the day in a rush. In her haste, Sarah burns the toast and Tom leaves his dirty clothes all over the floor as he dashes down to breakfast, wearing his least favourite shirt because the ironing is still awaiting Sarah's attention (her job). At this point neither say anything but both already have two items in their respective gunny-sacks. After breakfast Tom grinds his teeth because Sarah has squeezed the toothpaste tube in the middle — again; Sarah simmers because the shower is clogged up with hairs and the shampoo bottle is minus its cap and gets knocked over. The gunny-sacks become heavier. And so it goes on for several days with problems at work, pressures from the children and a sharp short phone call from Granny because they have forgotten to enquire about her trip to the doctor's, all adding weight to those invisible bags. Inevitably Tom and Sarah end up quite bent over with the weight on their shoulders, taking a very distorted view of life. Eventually, they go to push one more problem into the gunny-sack and it gives at the seams, so that all the grievances come tumbling out in a first class row!

That isn't the biblical solution! We need to deal with grievances when they come up if we can, and if that is not possible immediately, at least very soon after the event. Otherwise we end up with a relationship that resembles my refrigerator when it's in need of defrosting — full of little bits of left-overs that I've intended to use up, which, having got pushed to the back of the shelves, are now distinctly nasty! And if you're not sure how to bring the subject up again, try, 'I've been thinking about what happened the other day when . . .', or 'You know what you said about . . .' or simply 'I've got a problem!'

3. ATTACK THE PROBLEM, NOT YOUR PARTNER

Harmful words come to our minds so much more readily than helpful ones when we're angry, don't they? And most rows start on what is quite a minor point and then gather speed and momentum like a snowball rolling downhill. You'll see what I mean if you imagine the conversation when Sarah and Tom are emptying their gunny-sacks all over each other.

Sarah starts it when she says, 'I hope you're going to make sure that you set the alarm tonight. I don't want another morning like Monday.'

'Well, if you would get to bed instead of spending hours prinking and preening in the bathroom we wouldn't be so tired that we'd depend on the alarm,' Tom replies.

'At least I leave the bathroom tidy. It was disgusting when you left this morning and so was the bedroom.'

'If you'd had my blue shirt ironed, I wouldn't have had to spend ages looking for another one; there wasn't time to tidy up. Anyway we agreed that that was your job.'

'I'll do my jobs around the house when you see that yours are done. You've been out every night this week; what's the point of keeping the house nice if you're never here to appreciate it?' AND SO ON AND ON AND ON!

An 'I' message might be difficult to discipline yourself to in this kind of situation but go through that conversation exchanging 'I' for 'You,' and I think you will appreciate the difference it would make.

Harmful words degrade and destroy the dignity of the person you are talking to; they tear down his spirits and his self-esteem. There may be times when criticism is necessary, but it also needs to be constructive, truthful and spoken in love. Ask yourself — is it appropriate to say this at this moment? Some of us have a tendency to blurt things out without thinking. A lot of damage would be prevented if we would habitually ask ourselves, 'This may need to be said, but does it need saying now?'

Helpful words don't exaggerate — 'You always . . .', 'You never . . .'

Nor do they hit below the belt; bringing up old injuries from the past, or homing in on weak spots that you know he is struggling to deal with. When we are seeking the good of the other person we will refrain from brow-beating one another with verbal assault, or uncontrolled temper. We will not manipulate by using tears as a weapon or punish by withdrawing into long periods of silence, witholding sex, or doing other things that are in our power to make life uncomfortable. And let's not speak for each other by interrupting with, 'you don't mean that', 'what you're really saying is . . .'

4. BE KIND . . . AND TENDER-HEARTED . . . AND FORGIVING

Those words don't reflect the attitude of most of us when we are in a conflict situation, do they? We tend to rush in with guns blazing, stoutly defending our point of view at any cost, and the result is often damaged relationships and entrenched positions. So even if we feel that right is on our side it is worth trying to tackle the problem in God's way. God's way is to listen and love and forgive over and over again, and only he can help us to handle our anger like that. He never holds grudges or throws past mistakes back in our face. When he forgives, he forgets and we, too, should be forgiving people, remembering at all times how much we have been forgiven. Some of us find it very hard to let a bone of contention go. Like a dog we have an overwhelming desire to return to it for another little nibble. But Jesus said that we should put things right between ourselves and then consider the matter closed (Matt. 5.23). Grudges are like acid which will corrode and eventually destroy a relationship. Let them drop! Are you willing to forgive without 'ifs' and 'buts' — am I? And are you ready to put that forgiveness into words, because that is important?

Tricia was expecting her tenth baby, a fact that she was having some difficulty in coming to terms with. 'Don't you know that there are other ways of being creative?' joked one of her friends thoughtlessly on hearing the news. Then she sensed Tricia's hurt and quickly apologised. As we too often do, Tricia smiled and shrugged off the incident, but a little later Barbie returned to the subject. 'Please say that you forgive me for that tactless remark,' she said. 'Oh, it's all right,' said Tricia.

'No, it's important that you say "I forgive you",' insisted Barbie, 'or this will become unfinished business between us.'

And quite suddenly Tricia realised that she was right. Those words of dismissal hadn't really cleared the incident from her mind. But when she spoke the words of forgiveness and meant them, the incident was put where it belonged — in the past, and the sting had been taken from it because it had been forgiven.

One Christian writer of long ago said this about the formation of a natural pearl:

'Something comes into the world of the oyster that intrudes, and hinders and injures . . . but the pearl is the answer, by the injured, to the injury done.'

Since I heard that, I have been asking myself, 'Are the conflicts and problems in my life producing pearls or ulcers?' It is very much in my hands, for it all depends on the reaction by the injured to the injury done.

Points to ponder when conflict arises

1. What does this problem teach me about myself?
2. What does it show me about my partner?
3. What does it reveal about our relationship?
4. Is it producing pearls or ulcers?

Checking our route — Where have we gotten to so far?
A communication summary
What is communication?

We are all communicating with each other, all the time, whether we realise it or not.

Good communication occurs when the message that we want to transmit is received clearly and is understood.

Poor communication occurs when the message becomes distorted and is not understood.

How do we communicate?

We communicate with our words, through our senses, emotions and actions.

In order for communication to take place we must have a transmitter, a message to send and a receiver.

The message can become distorted when it passes through our in-built filters and when the transmitter or receiver develops faults.

What are the vital ingredients for good communication?

We must be prepared to:

    take risks
    face our fears
    pull down barriers
    understand and accept ourselves and the one to whom we want
      to communicate

Communication takes:

        time   patience
        courage   an open mind
        love

How do I bridge the gap between us?

We build bridges by:

    learning to talk and use 'I' messages
    learning how to listen and reflect back

learning how to use our senses to interpret non-verbal signs
learning my natural language of communication and how to distinguish that of others

How do we deal with conflict?

We need to deal with conflict by:

being truthful
dealing with anger correctly and constructively
using words that help rather than harm
being prepared to be kind, tender-hearted and forgiving

What is your communication quotient?

1. I pray for wisdom and discernment in our relationship
   usually   sometimes   never

2. I talk *to* my husband and not *at* him
   usually   sometimes   never

3. I understand my partner's primary language of communication and both use it and respond to it
   usually   sometimes   never

4. I can talk knowledgeably about his interests and share at least some of them
   usually   sometimes   never

5. I try to be open and honest and fully share my thoughts and opinions with him
   usually   sometimes   never

6. I accept and respect his silence when he doesn't speak
   usually   sometimes   never

7. I am sensitive to his needs of the moment and consider his feelings before I talk to him
   usually   sometimes   never

8. I tell my husband when I disagree and why
   usually   sometimes   never

9. I am as quick to compliment as I am to criticise
   usually   sometimes   never

10. When we have to discuss a problem I use 'I' messages rather than 'You' messages whenever possible
    usually   sometimes   never

11. My aim in our communication is as much to understand his point of view as it is to make sure that he understands mine
    usually   sometimes   never

12. I am a reflective listener
    usually   sometimes   never

Score 3 for usually
      1 for sometimes
      0 for never

If you scored 30+ — you're communicating
              20–30 — you're trying hard
              less than 20 — what a good job you bought this book!

10: Please Tell Me How You Feel

'There must be an emotional clearance between two involved partners in a love-relationship before they can safely enter into a discussion about plans, choices, values.'
JOHN POWELL

The psychologists who specialise in marital relationships say that every marriage has three phases. The first is the Honeymoon phase where romantic love gives a glow to everything and husband and wife float along on a cloud of togetherness (touching down very occasionally for a minor difference of opinion which is rapidly resolved). This may last as short a time as five weeks or as long as five years — and for most of us somewhere in the middle of that period.

After this comes the Facing Reality phase where the faults and the flaws begin to come into sharp focus and we begin to react with a few unobtrusive (we hope) attempts at remodelling our partner to get him closer to our specifications. When this doesn't happen, conflict and confrontation follow. The third phase might be called Make or Break — we either give up at this point and face a life of continual arguments, increasing estrangement or even divorce, or start to make attempts to adjust to reality and do the very best we can with it.

These three phases take place in the experience of every couple to a greater or lesser degree. In addition to this formost of us life goes a full circle with four stages in marriage. It starts with JUST THE TWO OF US; goes on to the YOUNG FAMILY stage and the GROWING FAMILY and then comes the EMPTY NEST when we're back to JUST THE TWO OF US again.

There have been many surveys and studies done into which areas in our lives contain the potential trouble spots, and although they are defined in different ways according to the approach taken, there are essentially eight basic areas that need our attention and that we, therefore, need to communicate about. We will consider each of these areas in the chapters that follows. They are —

1. How we are feeling about ourselves and each other.
2. Who decides what and how we do it.
3. What we want from our life together.
4. Where are we going and how we will get there.
5. How we spend our money.
6. How we express our love.
7. How we cope with our children and wider family relationships.
8. How we understand the spiritual dimension in our lives.

In the various books that I have read, lectures that I have listened to and conversations that I have had, while trying to discover more about communication, a great deal has been said and written (usually by men!) about the need of women to express their emotions, worries and fears and rather less about the needs of men (perhaps they don't have time to stop and think about their own needs because they're so busy analysing us!).

There are of course certain basic spiritual, physical, mental and emotional needs that are common to both sexes and a few that seem to be the particular concern of either men or women. And just to keep us on our toes that bit more, our personal needs and our joint needs tend to vary in the different phases and stages of marriage. We need to keep awake to this fact and be ready to meet the needs or give answers to the questions that our partners are asking today (not the ones that they were asking last month or will be asking in five years' time!). In the realm of feeling and emotion these questions will crop up again and again.

'Am I important to you?'

She was beautiful. Even in head and shoulders close-up on the television screen every feature was flawless, but as she gazed into the handsome hero's eyes she said something which, to me at least, was totally unexpected. 'When I'm with you I feel good about myself!' When I'm *with you* I feel good . . . which, by implication at least, suggested that when she was alone, she had doubts, beauty not withstanding.

'I feel good about myself'. This is one of the permanent needs that we all have, and since one of the main ways that we see ourselves is in relation to how others respond to us, we all need to hear warm words of appreciation and admiration spoken. We may not have the courage or perception to ask 'Am I a good husband; the kind of wife you want; am I meeting your needs as a provider; how am I doing as a parent?' but we all want to hear 'You're doing a great job' (even if there are a few suggestions for improvement tagged on!). And we all want to know that we are loved and accepted for what we are — warts and all. I think that one of the nicest things that Gordon has ever said to me was when I was bewailing the fact that I hadn't stuck to my diet (a boringly frequent occurrence!). Instead of agreeing that I was hopeless, weak-willed and a total failure he simply hugged me and said, 'I'm glad you're a fallible human being like me. Perfection would be impossible to live with!'

Another vital need we all share is to feel important to someone and needed. We have this need all the time but it requires more reinforcing at certain times, and in certain people. Women in particular it seems, often suffer from low self-esteem and can easily feel, especially in that 'Empty Nest' stage of marriage, that their usefulness is over, no one needs them any more. The technical term for this need to feel important to someone is centricity, and it must be met. We may do it with words: 'I don't know how I would manage without you', but those words need to be supported by our actions. If a husband seems to have time for anything and everything except his wife and her concerns, or a wife is totally pre-occupied with the home, her children or her job, words, however complimentary, won't mean very much. A couple like that may not realise the reason for their resentment, but when they argue about the long hours he works or spends on his hobbies, or the fact that the wife is too house-proud or spoils the children, they are saying in effect, 'Are these things or people more important to you than I am?'

If you have arguments along these lines, ask yourself, 'What are we really saying?

'Am I saying one thing with words and another thing with my actions? What have either of us done in the last month which says, "You are important to me. Your affairs and interests come high on my list of priorities"?'

Remember, when someone feels secure in this area, he or she can cope with separation, time pressures and the demands of others with comparative ease. But if this sense of significance and purpose is missing, we are likely to make more and more frantic efforts to secure it, or else to sink down into apathy and despair.

Lorna's laughter was close to tears when she said, 'Gary gave me a pretty clear picture of my priority rating when I had an accident in the car last week. When I phoned his office to tell him, his first question was, 'How is the car?'

his second was, 'Are the children OK?' eventually he said, 'How about you?'

Do you love me?

We have already considered the fact that we use different languages of communication to express love, but most of us need to hear 'I love you' in words as well as actions from time to time. Men in particular seem to find it hard to say those three words that many women yearn to hear. This is partly because, in general, men use words to express ideas and to share information, whereas women use them to reveal feelings and emotions. When a woman says to her husband, 'Do you love me?' and he replies 'You know I do' that is quite true. She usually does know. But she has a very real need to hear him say it. And although her husband may not admit it, she is not alone. Little boys have just as much of a need to know that they are loved and precious as any little girl, and so do their fathers and grandfathers. In spite of all the changes in the way we do things there is still a tendency to think of men as the wooers and women as the wooed, and perhaps it is at this point that there is a need to give equality a chance! The old saying 'There is always one who kisses and one who holds the cheek' may be true, but it doesn't always have to be the *same* one. Both partners need to hear love expressed, and if you have real difficulty with words spoken, words written down in the form of a note, a card or a poem (your own or someone else's) can often untie your tongue. 'I love you' in any language and at any age gives a glow around the heart, so let's spell it out in every way and on any occasion that creative caring can devise.

What do you want from me?

Has it ever struck you that we can spend years trying to fulfil expectations and requirements that we *think* other people have for us, only to discover that they exist only in our imagination? On the other hand, we may not be fulfilling hopes that they do have of us, because we don't know what they are. Greg and Mary did that.

When they first met and married, Greg was an outwardly successful young businessman who appeared to be destined for a seat on the board of his company. Mary gave the impression of being competent rather than ambitious, but underneath this facade she was a creative and able girl with career dreams of her own. However, Mary assumed that Greg expected her to support his career (that was what *her* mother had done for *her* father and somehow she and Greg never really discussed that kind of thing), and so she put her own dreams aside She tried valiantly to settle down at home and be a 'Company' wife, to cope serenely with Greg's absences overseas and be ready to socialise and entertain in order to improve his promotion prospects. At times she felt like a fish out of water, but she battled on without complaint because she loved Greg and wanted to be the kind of wife he needed. So it came as rather a shock when, eight years after they were married, Greg announced that he was sick of business life, that he had only gone into his profession because his parents had insisted, and stayed in it because Mary seemed to like the life they led. But he couldn't stand it any longer. Now he wanted to live on a croft in the Outer Hebrides and paint landscapes!

Poor Mary! At first she was hurt and angry. All her sacrifices seemed to have been for nothing. But Greg's honesty, although shattering for them both at first, transformed their lives. You see, once they really talked about what they wanted for themselves and each other, they no longer had to fit in with an imaginary standardised picture, and could set about creating the partnership and life-style that they both wanted. Consequently, they compromised on the Outer Hebrides, and moved to rural Sussex instead. There, Greg taught part-time, painted his landscapes (and discovered a talent for portraits too!) and Mary developed her own business skills by opening a shop in which she sold Greg's and other rural craftsmen's work.

If you have never talked these kind of things through, or perhaps haven't done so recently, you might like to ask yourself and your partner —

1. What kind of qualities am I looking for in you at the moment to support me/fulfil my need?
2. Is the lifestyle that we have today as satisfying to us both as it was two, five, or ten years ago?
3. Am I asking you to do things or be something that is not really 'you' because I have a stereotype picture of what husbands/wives of a certain age and in a particular situation should be like?

What are you afraid of?

We have already discussed fears in some detail but it is helpful to expand a little further at this point, because again fears and our need to talk about them or deal with them, do vary from stage to stage in our lives.

One of the commonest fears as we go on through life is one of getting older. Women are afraid of losing their looks, their children and their husbands. Men fear losing their attractiveness to the opposite sex too, and they often feel threatened if their wives develop new interests or skills in which they are not included. A wife's return to paid employment may be seen as a threat, as well as a boost to the family budget. And when it comes to employment, other fears of being overtaken in their jobs or even losing their jobs altogether can cast a real shadow over their lives. In fact, fear of failure in any realm is said to be the ultimate fear for most men. How can we deal with this? As with any fear, it grows darker when it lurks, half hidden in the dark corners of our minds, so bring it out. Let's talk about it and make sensible provision for the fact that we are all growing older and need to take care of our bodies as well as our minds and spirits; that children do leave home and that a life-time's career will, one day, cease to fill every waking hour. If we ask ourselves 'what particular joys and opportunities does this phase of life bring with it, both for me as an individual and for us as a couple?' we will enjoy the now, instead of gazing wistfully back at the past. Then we can regard these events as doorways to freedom instead of the gates of a prison, and they will lose their power to frighten us.

Another thing that many people fear is showing too much emotion. Penny refuses to discuss any sensitive subjects with her husband because once he broke down and cried and Penny is terrified that he will do it again. Linda used to refuse to do the same because *she* is easily moved to tears and she was afraid of her husband's reaction. But when her husband demonstrated that he wasn't disturbed by her tears and they both reached the point where they could laugh at the fact that he always had a spare handkerchief in his pocket, she was able to relax and be open with him.

Emotions are God's gift to us, they give light and shade to life. The Bible tells us that Jesus wept — but he also joined in feasts and merry-making; he was angry with exploiters and hypocrites and unembarrassed by an extravagant demonstration of love. So let's be open with each other, ready to accept both laughter and tears, anger and affection for what they are. The Psalmist says, 'I prayed to the Lord, and he answered me; he freed me from all my fears' (Ps. 34.4). God can set us free in this area as in all others, if we will allow him to do so. So face the fears. Ask yourself —

1. What am I afraid of today?
2. Have I expressed this fear to my partner and asked him to help dispel it?
3. Have I expressed this fear to God?
4. What is my partner afraid of deep down?
5. How can I help him to deal with it? Does he need a sympathetic listener, supportive action, or a change in behaviour on my part?

And one general question —

6. How do I rate the way we share on a 'feelings' level — scale 1 to 10? If I'm not very satisfied what can I do about it?

11: Decisions, Decisions, Decisions!

'Communication is at its best when two people mutually serve one another in love, each reaching out to the need of the other.'

It was Helen Keller who said, 'Life is an exciting business and most exciting when it is lived for others'. If that is true, marriage and family living should be pretty exciting, for in these relationships above all we have the opportunity to live for other people right down the line. Some people say that marriage should be a 50–50 proposition; an American president's wife suggested 70–30; Dr John Bettler goes 30% further! He says that when you are *both* prepared to give 100% then you have the basis for a good marriage.

In the course of the Anglican marriage service the minister speaks of the couple making a covenant or bargain. In entering into most bargains we want to know, 'Is what I'm getting worth what I'm giving up?' But the biblical view of marriage is that we should covenant to be a bargain, rather than to get one! And that is something that doesn't come naturally!

Ephesians 5.24–33 is one of the most analysed, criticised and hotly debated sections of Paul's writings (among women at least) and has caused many a 'thoroughly modern Millie' to call his motives and his meaning into question. But really Paul is calling both husbands and wives to live a life of love and submission to one another; both are being asked to give 100%. It is the way in which this is done that is looked at differently. For while both men and women are equal in God's sight, both heirs of his gifts of life, within marriage the husband has been given the responsibility of being the one with whom the buck eventually stops. But this doesn't give him the 'King Complex' — or it shouldn't!

For Paul is quick to point out that a man's attitude to his wife should be the same as that of Jesus Christ to *his* bride, the church, and think what that was like! Jesus loved the Church, to the point of laying down his life for her, and that love goes on and on as he cherishes her and aims to make her the most beautiful expression of his love that she can be, reaching her full potential.

The wife's side sounds harder — but is it really? She is to submit to her husband's leadership; in other words to choose to be a bargain and to give herself 100% in being a helpmate. Note that I said 'choose'. True submission is a voluntary thing. It is an attitude of the heart, not just of certain actions, and that can't be dragged from me by force. But it transforms relationships, taking away all the elbowing for advantage and one-upmanship. Jesus said, 'If you cling to your life you will lose it; but if you give it up for me you will save it' (Matt. 10.39, LB) and the same applies to our rights. Cling on to them and put 'me' first and disaster follows as sure as night comes after day. God intended marriage to give completion to the two individuals involved, not competition.

But what, you might ask, has this got to do with communication? A great deal, when you come to sort out how you will tackle decision-making and to discuss your ideas about male and female roles in marriage. You see, many people get confused about this idea of headship and submission when it comes to working it out in practical terms. Some men take the position that their marriage relationship should be of the Dictator-Doormat variety with them giving the orders and their wives meekly carrying them out without a word. Others talk a lot about it and make no attempt to actually take any responsibility; not surprisingly that doesn't go down too well with their wives either! Some couples see it as something to do with who does the washing up and who looks after the children. But that is cultural conditioning and not biblical principle!

And women are at fault too. Some of us equate submission with never having to think for ourselves again; others fight dirty — appearing to submit but undermining his attempts to take responsibility at every turn. None of these attitudes has anything to do with the biblical view at all. So if these are some of the ways in which you are dealing with decision making, think again. Facing the situation realistically, most couples reach their decisions by discussion and compromise, and that is good. But there has to be a way of dealing with things when a stalemate is reached and a decision *has* to be made, and it is then that a wife is required to submit to her husband's leadership and, having stated her case, leaves the responsibility for the final decision to him with a smile (and no recriminations later)! If you are both intent on giving 100% the situation won't arise very often!

Having an agreed definition of this matter of authority in the marriage relationship gives us a firm foundation but it doesn't solve all our problems over decision making and male/female responsibilities in marriage of course. Each couple will need to talk these through for themselves and reassess the situation from time to time.

Who decides what and how?

Some couples divide responsibility so that she decides all the day to day matters that apply to the home, while he takes care of things that go on in the world outside their four walls. Others are like George and Janet.

'When we got married,' joked George at his silver wedding celebration, 'Janet and I agreed that I would make all the big decisions and she would take care of the minor ones. I'm glad to report that so far, in 25 years of marriage, we've had no big decisions to make!'

Have you got an agreed formula for decision making in your relationship? One couple that I know, who both have demanding careers and little time together, actually make a formal agenda which they 'issue' some days before they plan a decision making session, and treat the whole process as formally as they do their work decisions. Esther and Steve would laugh at that but they could learn a few lessons from them nonetheless — they never decide about anything until the deadline is staring them in the face, and then, because they decide in haste, they often repent at leisure!

So ask yourself: Who makes most of the day to day decisions? Would your partner and children agree with the answer you gave to that question? And have the children discovered that they can get their way by playing one of you off against the other? (You wouldn't, of course, dream of using your children to twist your partner's arm, would you?) And if you decide on the major/minor decision split, how do you distinguish between the two?

What is your opinion about what a man does in marriage and what a woman does — and does this tally with your partner's view? How do you decide on the responsibility for household chores for instance? Is it on the basis of what you have a natural inclination for and what you enjoy doing, or the way your parents always did things? I don't recall seeing my father-in-law in the kitchen overmuch, certainly not doing the cooking anyway, but when we had three under-fives Gordon felt that a spell of peace and quiet in the kitchen getting the breakfast ready was infinitely preferable to the tricky task of coaxing three small bodies into their clothes. This habit has continued (although nowadays I'm putting the finishing touches to six packed lunches!) and although some of our friends tease us about it, we worry not. It suits us and it suits our life-style and that is the important thing!

One major point we need to recognize in our decision making is something called couple-pace. Some people find it very easy to come to a decision. They are clear-sighted, decisive and perhaps somewhat impatient or impetuous. Others are cautious, and analytical, liking to look at the problem from every aspect, listing all the options and their advantages and disadvantages and weighing the whole matter very carefully. When a quick decision maker is married to a slow one, fireworks are likely!

One of three things may happen. Firstly the rapid thinker may force his opinions through, and, because he seems to have it all cut and dried, the slower partner feels too inhibited to have his/her say, but simply waits until the decision is made and then approves or disapproves of it (and often smoulders with resentment for a long time afterwards).

Secondly, the slower partner may insist on doing things his/her way, implying that he is the really thoughtful and reliable one and the other is rash and liable to make mistakes — and nearly drives the quicker thinker mad with frustration or to sleep with boredom. Or thirdly, the fast decision maker learns to slow down, the slow partner makes a deliberate effort to speed up, and they decide on a time scale which is acceptable to them both. This is something that we have learned to do because if I don't really think and talk things through to my satisfaction I tend to feel uncertain and unsettled about any decision we make. Gordon finds this exasperating (especially as we very often come back to his 'instant' solution!) but we have found that a preliminary chat, a pause to think things over and then a decision making session relieves the pressure on us both.

What do we have to decide about?

There are dozens of decisions that we take day by day and we hardly notice that we have made them. But in every relationship there are major decisions to be faced from time to time about our homes and families; annual events like holidays and budgeting for the year ahead, and life changes such as a new job, moving house or adding to the family. We need to recognise that all major changes do bring a degree of stress in their wake even if they are pleasant ones. (I never expected to be made miserable by having a lovely new kitchen, but living without it for nearly three weeks and then not being able to find anything in the new streamlined set up was quite a shock to the system!)

A loving partner realises that stress does need to be recognised, accepted and talked through (not ignored or laughed away) if it is to be dealt with satisfactorily, even if it seems to be a minor matter to the one who is not directly involved. And if one or both of you are in a stressful situation then all decisions, other than those related to the problem in hand, are best shelved for the time being if that is possible.

Check it out?

Perhaps you sail through decision making as smoothly as a knife cuts through butter! If so, pass over the next chapter. But if, like most of us, you have difficulties or conflict over coming to decisions, at least some of the time, ask yourself and your partner —

1. Are we working out a truly biblical pattern of authority in our marriage, or are we super-imposing our own or other people's ideas?
2. Do we know and accept each other's decision making 'pace' and have we worked out a method to suit us both?
3. Do I approach a decision with the thought, 'How can I make it easy for us to reach the right decision?' or am I humming under my breath 'We'll do this *my* way'?
4. How do I rate our decision making skills on a scale 1–10? If the score is low what can I do to improve things?

12: Competition or Completion?

' "This is it!" Adam exclaimed. "She is part of my own bone and flesh. Her name is 'woman' because she was taken out of a man. This explains why a man leaves his father and mother and is joined to his wife in such a way that the two become one person." ' (Gen 2.23, 24, LB)
' . . . Let there be spaces in your togetherness, And let the winds of heaven dance between you. Love one another, but make not a bond of love.' KAHLIL GIBRAN

Today marriages are breaking down at a more rapid rate than ever before, and many and varied are the reasons that the experts put forward for this happening. Like many expert opinions they differ widely, but one theme that comes up again and again is to do with our expectations of marriage. Some people pitch their expectations very high. They have swallowed the fairy tales hook, line and sinker, and expect to live happily ever after with no particular effort on their part. Others have a rather cynical view and enter the relationship with a convenient termination clause in the back of their minds — 'if it doesn't work out, divorce is there pretty much for the asking'. And many of us have never really crystallised what we expect or hope for, and yet go through life with a niggling sense of disillusionment and dissatisfaction.

So it is important that we should ask ourselves individually and as a couple, 'What do we want from our life together? What are we prepared to do to turn dreams into reality?' These questions need to be asked before we enter a permanent relationship but they also need to be repeated at intervals afterwards. As we move from phase to phase and stage to stage in marriage our aspirations and therefore our answers will vary. Some will be fairly obvious — creating a home and perhaps a family, deciding on a life-style and so on, and we will discuss these in more detail later. But there is a very basic consideration that underlies all the rest, and yet may never have entered your mind, and that is 'How involved am I prepared to get in your life and how involed do I want you to become in mine?'

'Surely,' said Leonie, when we were discussing this, 'the whole point of marriage is total involvement — the two becoming one flesh and all that. If you have less, it's not really marriage! It's all there in Genesis 2 after all.'

How do you feel about that statement? It is certainly true that God's ideal was that the first man and woman should complete each other's needs and form the perfect whole, but in a less than perfect world, this is often an ideal state to be worked towards, rather than to be slipped on with the wedding rings.

Marriage counsellors Vera and David Mace describe three levels of involvement in marriage which can be illustrated in diagrammatic form like this:

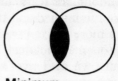

| Maximum involvement | Limited involvement | Minimum involvement |

Maximum involvement means that you each keep some degree of individuality, but your lives overlap to a very large extent. Minimum involvement suggests two people living pretty separate lives but obtaining a degree of pleasure and comfort from sharing some things together, and limited involvement as the diagram shows, comes somewhere in the middle. Which category would you say that your relationship falls into, and are you happy with the situation?

Personal privacy and space

We have varying needs for privacy and space within the close quarters of marriage, and men in particular sometimes seem to find their wives' desire for a large degree of 'togetherness' stifling to the point of feeling smothered. Trevor was like that. He came from a family of individualists where it was taken for granted that they would do their own thing — to a destructive degree when it came to any sense of being a family. His wife Catherine was from a very close-knit family who phoned each other weekly, and both expected and enjoyed frequent get-togethers. Catherine assumed that this attitude would be uppermost in her own marriage and when Trevor wanted to go fishing — alone — or walked for miles with only the dog for company she felt unloved and unwanted. In actual fact, this was no reflection on his feelings; Trevor loved her dearly but just needed this space in the midst of a very busy life to be himself and by himself from time to time. When Catherine realised this and made up her mind to accept it and to let him go without grumbling or tears, his need for long periods of time on his own diminished and they were able to move closer together in a more relaxed way.

You may not feel quite such an urgent need to be on your own as Trevor, but many women, especially if they have young children, have an occasional overwhelming desire to think their own thoughts without interruption for a change! When our older children were pre-schoolers I couldn't understand why I was getting so bad tempered with everyone — until I realised that because our youngest had given up her daytime nap rather sooner than her brothers I was experiencing for the first time what it was like *never* to have a silent minute in the day! And husbands, too, often need a few minutes of quietness in which to switch over from work to family matters when they get home at the end of the day. This isn't always easy to provide when there is a hungry horde waiting to be fed, or little ones to be dealt with, but let's not be afraid of admitting these needs to one another. They should not be seen as threats to our relationship, but as an opportunity to give what we can with understanding and love.

The right to my own opinions

Of course, it isn't only in the realm of time spent alone that this need for privacy is expressed. Many of us, especially if we are still a little insecure, and uncertain of ourselves, need space to hold our own opinions and think our own thoughts without being argued with or persuaded to think otherwise by our partners.

'Bill never talks to me nowadays about his work,' complained Yvonne. 'When we were first married he did discuss things with me, but he didn't like it when I made suggestions, and he would never admit that any of my ideas were good ones. In fact he got quite angry once or twice and told me that I didn't understand the situation!' 'He didn't like it when I made suggestions' — Yvonne had the answer to the problem in her own hands, although she couldn't recognise it without help. She was a very creative individual, who would brainstorm a whole list of ideas and solutions to any given problem within minutes of being presented with it. Bill was quieter, less confident, a more deliberate thinker, and when Yvonne turned her creativity onto his concerns he turned off! When she realised that he felt threatened by her spate of ideas, she took the bull by the horns and promised not to suggest anything unless he asked her to. As a result, he began to talk again; she listened with resolutely buttoned lips, and eventually he invited her comments — which she gave in small quantities and with a total determination not to become ruffled if he ignored the lot!

In a way, Yvonne and Bill's problem was more easily dealt with than some others — she had to refrain from giving advice unless asked for it. An even more sensitive area comes in the realm of beliefs that we hold dear, especially in the spiritual realm. There is a real temptation to try and put our partner right, especially if we hold differing views on some point of doctrine (or one is a believer and one is a non-believer) which we think is vital to the faith.

Now I am not suggesting that it doesn't matter what we believe so long as we're sincere, or that we shouldn't have a clear grasp of what our faith teaches, but it is no use battering someone else over the head with your Bible (figuratively speaking) or trying subtle brain-washing techniques by playing tapes of your favourite preacher's brilliant sermon on the point at issue, at maximum volume! To be sure the apostle Peter did instruct us to 'Always be prepared to give an answer to everyone who *asks* you to give a reason for the hope that you have. But do this with *gentleness* and *respect*' (1 Pet. 3.15). There are three key words in those two sentences. We give an answer when *asked* for it, and we do it *gently*, with respect for the other's right to hold their own opinions. We do not make our acceptance and love for them as *people* conditional on their sharing our views. We need to remember at all times that it is the Holy Spirit's job to convict and convince, and if he wants our help he will let us know!

Keep off my turf

Territorial aggression sounds more like a skirmish between two opposing armies than a reaction of two people who love each other, doesn't it? But if you have ever sat behind a man who is in the passenger seat of the car, when he feels that it is his place to be behind the wheel, you'll appreciate the phrase! We all have some areas of our lives that we feel to be our particular responsibility, and if we are slightly aggressive by nature, or maybe feel insecure about our performance in this particular realm we are likely to get very edgy if anyone intrudes, however well-meaningly.

Andy and Faith are a good case in point. Faith is a full-time homemaker, who is not cut out for domesticity by nature, but is not convinced that she is cut out for anything else either! So she is rather defensive about her performance in the home, and she feels that Andy is secretly comparing her with his mom, who is one of the real earth-mother types! Washing and ironing are her chief bugbears; she never seems to have an empty laundry basket for more than half a day at a time.

One Saturday Andy had been playing in a football match and came home feeling somewhat guilty about the carry-all full of dirty clothes that Faith was going to find on her return from shopping. Then he had what seemed at the time to be a brilliant idea. He would wash them himself and, what is more, he would take some of the other laundry from the basket to make up a full load. He sorted the colors out carefully (his mother had trained him well!) and when Faith came home she was greeted by a beaming Andy with a pile of washed and neatly folded clothes. They then had the biggest row of their entire marriage! Faith thought that this was a subtle way of getting at her for her incompetence, and Andy was quite genuinely hurt and mystified. But it had one good effect when the dust had settled a little — they talked! Andy realised that Faith needed her own territory and that he had to encourage her rather than take over from her. Faith learned, to her amazement, that Andy didn't really care how she ran the home as long as certain priorities were met and he certainly was not comparing her with anyone, least of all his mother. Life in general and their communication in particular was quite considerably improved after that episode!

Co-operation and teamwork

I wouldn't want you to run away with the idea, from Faith and Andy's story, that I am advocating not helping one another. One of the joys and strengths of any close relationship, and of marriage in particular, is co-operation and teamwork, and we shall explore this in detail in the next chapter. But the point at issue is that we offer help, advice, support and togetherness to the degree that we both want it at this moment. This will vary: sometimes more, sometimes less. There is no standard ideal level of involvement for all time that fits every couple. We need to ask ourselves —

1. What degree of involvement do we want at this present time?
2. What can I do (or refrain from doing) to make our relationship one of completion rather than competition?
3. Am I willing to make sacrifices in order to meet his needs in this area?
4. How satisfied am I about our level of life-overlap on a scale 1–10?

13: Strategy for Living

'Two people working together, can achieve more than either could individually, using the same amount of time and effort.'

'Marriage,' says the Anglican wedding service, 'is a holy

mystery in which man and woman become one flesh.' Some of us back away from that thought a little! After all, if we are to become one, which one out of the two of us ceases to exist? It can make marriage sound like a take-over bid! But I don't think that this is what is meant at all. Rather than a take-over of one personality by another, marriage is intended to be a merger, in which we compensate for each other's weaknesses, and are supported by one another's strengths. Some of this we do unconsciously; some of it needs thinking and talking through. For, as the authors of *No Fault Marriage** say,

> 'The amount of satisfaction you get from marriage is determined in large part by how well you and your partner agree to meet certain of each other's needs. It also depends on the degree of opportunity and encouragement you get from each other to meet some of your own needs.'

If we are to meet our own and each other's needs, we have to have some idea of what they are. We have already thought about how we might pin-point our own needs by asking ourselves, 'Where am I going?' in chapter 5. But if two of you get goals in isolation there can be problems. Ideally you need to know what you want to accomplish as an individual. You also need to know what your partner wants to do (and vice versa) and if there isn't to be a conflict of interests, these two lines of thinking have to be slotted into your plan for your life as a couple.

Some people have never really thought of setting goals for themselves, either jointly or individually, and if anyone suggests it to them, find the whole idea rather threatening or daunting. When Marcia asked her husband John what his goals were he groaned and said, 'Do I have any? All I want to do is retire!' Well, although he didn't recognise it as such, that was a goal! (And when they started to talk about why he was so disinterested in his job, and why he was finding life so burdensome, they uncovered a completely fresh view of their present life-style, that neither had been aware of.)

But is John right — are goals important or just an optional extra for the organised few? I would suggest that they are a big part of the answer to that feeling that life is tearing past and we have little to show for it. As the late Adlai Stevenson said, 'It's not the days of your life, but the life in your days that counts.' The apostle Paul would back him up on that now. In his letter to the church at Ephesus he writes, 'Live life . . . with a due sense of responsibility, not as men (and women) who do not know the meaning and purpose of life, but as those who do. Make the best use of your time despite all the difficulties of these days' (Eph. 5.15–16, Phillips).

What is important to you?

If we are to decide on our joint goals, we have to discover what is important to us, individually and together. For instance, imagine that the Jones family is going to France for their summer holiday. In their discussions about what to do and where to go, they have established that they all want to go abroad to somewhere that is sunny and warm. But they all have other priorities that they haven't talked about. Mr. Jones wants to explore the history of the area, Mrs. Jones wants to sample the local cooking, their son dreams of learning to windsurf, and their daughter hopes for an opportunity to practice her French. So when it becomes apparent that the area is a little short of ancient ruins, that the few local restaurants there are very expensive, and that their campsite has a large proportion of British visitors and no facilities for windsurfing, they are all rather disappointed with their long-awaited trip. And yet, if they had been more specific about what they wanted, a few adjustments in the basic plan would have seen them all catered for.

In the same way we may have lazy dreams about being successful, becoming better parents or a more vital Christian, but if we never stop to work out what we need to do in order to fulfil those dreams — and start to do it — we probably won't get very far. Obviously each couple will have different hopes and ambitions, which fit in with their particular temperaments and circumstances, but we all need to consider our lives in the general areas of spiritual and physical fitness, mental and emotional fitness and progress and achievement in our daily work. We should aim to provide an atmosphere in our relationship in which growth in all these areas is not only possible but actively encouraged.

1. SPIRITUAL AND PHYSICAL FITNESS

If we stop progressing in the spiritual realm we very soon start to slide backwards, and the same can be said of our physical fitness — if we cease to use our faculties we become weak and flabby and unfit. So spiritual and physical health are both very important, and this is an area in which we can really help each other. That is not to say that we can exercise spiritually or physically on each other's behalf, but Gordon can encourage me to maintain my personal relationship with God as my number one priority and to keep my body fit and trim and I can do the same for him, and we can look for opportunities to do these things together. When we are accountable to someone else, it is a great incentive to stay on the straight and narrow path. So if we agree that we each need to spend 15 minutes in Bible reading and prayer every morning and to take a certain amount of exercise each week (and check up at intervals to see how things are going!) we are far more likely to do it than if we struggle on unsupported.

And if we have the opportunity to undertake some joint responsibility in Christian work, let's give it our serious consideration, even if the thought terrifies us and we feel as if we would be stretched to the limit of our capacity. Facing a challenge like that, especially if we can do it together, is an excellent spur to spiritual growth and to a real sense of sharing and partnership.

2. MENTAL AND EMOTIONAL FITNESS

Our emotions are often linked with our goals. For instance, if we are uncertain about achieving something that we want to do very much, we may become anxious; if we are frustrated in our attempts to do something we may become angry, and if we set our sights too high and find it impossible to reach our goal we are very likely to become depressed. So we need to be realistic about our time, our talents and our circumstances in setting our goals.

And while we will obviously be looking for loving emotional support from our partner we also need to aim for a healthy degree of independence in the mental and emotional realm — not too much, not too little! Too many people rely on their husband or wife to meet *all* their needs in this area, and women in particular expect to find their total identity through their partner instead of developing their own personality. But we should, as Ruth Graham says, 'Allow your husband the privilege of being just a man. Don't expect him to read your mind and give you the security, the joy and the peace . . . that only God can give.'

We also need to allow for differences in our individual goals without getting annoyed or feeling threatened. For instance, if my husband was wondering whether to take a course on car maintenance which would occupy one evening each week, I could react in one of two ways. Either I could oppose the idea outwardly on the grounds that he didn't have the time, and inwardly because I didn't want him to have a skill that I did not and was afraid that he might become one of these men who spend all their time getting greasy under a car (I probably wouldn't mention either of the last two reasons). Or I could encourage him on the grounds that although it would be time-consuming in the short-term, it would save money and give him a new and very useful skill in the long-term. Therefore this goal that I couldn't share would enhance rather than threaten our marriage (so long as I had the right attitude to it).

In addition to our individual interests, we need to have interests that we share. Companionship is one of the essential ingredients of a good marriage, and although it requires compromise, effort and time, it is worth every minute we spend on it. Many couples who have problems in communication do very little together, and then wonder why they have little to communicate about! Relationship building activities have certain things in common —

a) they are activities you do rather than something that is done for you — i.e. making music together rather than going to a concert.

b) they are activities that make you aware of each other.

c) they are activities that give you the opportunity to talk. Don't worry if there is only one interest that you genuinely share and can do together. Make a start on that, and you will probably soon discover others.

3. PROGRESS AND ACHIEVEMENT IN OUR DAILY WORK

There is little else that is so deadening to a good relationship than for one person to be totally or even mildly disinterested in the interests and concerns that fill most of the other person's working day. Admittedly, the claims of work and home do sometimes conflict, but when a wife begins to regard her husband's work as her rival, or the husband feels the same about his wife's job or absorption in her home-making and care of the children, there's trouble ahead. Although it isn't easy, we need to understand and accept our partner's commitment to the job in hand and give our full support and encouragement for him to achieve his goals in this area (without trying to manoeuvre or manipulate him into doing more than he wants to or is able to handle). And the same is true of course, for the husband in regard to his wife. We need to ask ourselves 'Where does he or she need help? How may my pre-conceived ideas about the situation be blocking him or her from receiving the help needed?' Be very practical!

We have found that it is very difficult, if not impossible, for us both to be working at full stretch at the same time. So, if I am writing flat-out to meet a publisher's deadline, we try (not always successfully) to see that it is at a time when Gordon's job is not requiring more than routine attention, and if Gordon is extra busy or making major changes in practice organisation, I try to make sure that I am able to give him my support and relieve him from extra responsibility at home.

But how do you find the time?

'It's all very well to talk about goals and shared interests,' sighed Nancy, 'but our life is so hectic that we can't keep up with the things we're doing now, never mind looking for anything else to do.' I quite saw what *she* meant. She was the wife of a very busy business man, whose job involved a great deal of travel and entertaining. She had a part-time job which she did from home and four school age children. In addition to this, Nancy had an elderly aunt who needed daily visits and both she and Malcolm were actively involved in their local church. But Nancy had misunderstood what *I* meant! You see, setting goals for your life doesn't necessarily mean that you do more. In fact, it may well result in you doing less. In their book *Strategy for Living** the authors, who are time-management consultants, say this:

seek what it is God wants you to do and be —
   SET GOALS

discover which goals are more important —
   ESTABLISH PRIORITIES

analyse the best way to reach your goals —
   DO YOUR PLANNING

start working towards your goals according to your plans —
   START LIVING

Sometimes our lives are full just because we have never set goals and then decided on our priorities, and so our days have become cluttered up by commitments that are no longer relevant or by jobs that should have been given up or delegated to other people. If you feel that your life is in just that sort of tangle, you might like to use the chart that Nancy (and many other people) used to get her goals and priorities sorted out.

My present responsibilities 1.	Amount of time needed each day or week. 2.	How am I performing? 1–10 3.	Could anyone else do this? Yes/No/Maybe 4.	Priority rating ABC and action needed 5.

In column 1 Nancy listed every responsibility she had at present from personal spiritual growth through her secretarial responsibilities to the Parent Teacher Association, to keeping in touch with her brother in Africa and visiting and writing to his children at their English boarding school.

In column 2 she made a rough estimate of the time she spent on each responsibility and found that she ran out of hours in the week — which explained why she felt frayed at the edges! She found it salutary to note that some of the things that she gave an 'A' priority to, were in practice given the least time. Then she asked Malcolm to fill in a similar chart, noting down what *he* felt her responsibilities were, what her priorities should be and how she was performing. Then they did the same for him — he filled in a chart for himself and Nancy did one according to how *she* saw his life. They then discussed their findings, and a *very* revealing exercise that proved to be! As a result they delegated a number of items; cut out two or three altogether and added two that they both felt were important, and for which they now had time. Doing all this didn't change their life to one of calm tranquillity; they were still very busy. But having identified the trouble spots and danger areas they were more careful to think and pray before they agreed to do anything, and they had a sense of achieving something in their personal and family life because they knew what they were aiming to do and how they were intending to do it.

Christians are inevitably very busy people, for they have their church commitments to balance with the demands of home, work, family and other people. But it is no more spiritual to muddle through than to sit down and prayerfully think things through. We must always be prepared for God to show us that we need to change our plans, but with that proviso firmly in mind, let's ask ourselves —

1. Is our home a greenhouse or a desert as far as personal and joint growth is concerned?
2. Can I see any individual and/or joint progress in the areas of mental, emotional, physical and spiritual fitness during the last year?

3. Do I know what I am aiming to achieve in my daily work? Have I made plans to turn dreams into reality?
4. Do I know what goals my partner has for his life? Am I helping him to achieve them?
5. What are our joint goals for our lives together in relation to —

   a) our Christian commitment?

   b) our home and family?

   c) our hobbies and interests?

   d) our possessions?

Have we given priorities to these goals and are we making plans to reach them?

For further information on the subject of goal setting and time management you may like to read

— *Strategy for Living*★ by Edward R. Dayton and Ted W. Engstrom

— *How do You Find the Time*★ by Pat King;

— *How to get Control of Your Time and Your Life*★ by Alan Lakein.

14: Money Talks!

'*You cannot serve two masters: God and money. For you will hate one and love the other, or else the other way around. So my counsel is: don't worry about things — food, drink, money and clothes . . . Will all your worries add a single moment to your life? . . . don't worry at all about having enough food and clothing . . . your heavenly Father already knows perfectly well that you need them. And he will gladly give them to you if you give him first place in your life.*' (*Selections from Matt. 6.24–33*).

'The only thing that money says to us is "goodbye"!' sighed Sandra. 'I know the feeling,' agreed Jean, 'and for some reason, it's the main thing that Douglas and I argue about. I suppose it's because we've got such different attitudes to the way that money should be handled. I sometimes feel we'll never find a way to talk about it without losing our cool, although we've managed to do it with most other touchy subjects.'

It's a rare marriage that doesn't have a few hiccoughs about financial matters, but in some circumstances the hiccoughs are more like convulsions and threaten to pull the fabric of the whole relationship to pieces. And like any other sensitive subject we often find it very difficult to communicate how we feel without conflict.

Jean put her finger on one of the root causes of their problems when she pointed out that she and Douglas had different basic attitudes to money and possessions, formed by their home backgrounds to a very large extent. Jean's parents were not wealthy but she was an only child and all her childhood needs and many of her 'wants' had been supplied without any questions asked. Douglas, on the other hand, was the eldest of four brothers and his parents had had to count every penny as well as being by nature rather puritanical folk. They always asked before deciding on any potential purchase, not 'Do we need it?' but 'Can we do without it?' — and the answer to that was usually 'yes'! Douglas had absorbed that attitude as part of his upbringing and so he found Jean's approach to possessions, which broadly speaking was 'Do we need it? Can we pay for it? Why not get it?' at best frivolous and at worst downright infuriating!

What is our starting point?

In communicating with our partners about money matters, this is the first question we need to ask ourselves —

'What is his basic attitude towards finance and material possessions, and is this a result of the influence of his home background or his rebellion against it?'

Remember that often we are determined not to repeat what we regard as our parents' mistakes and as a result, swing right round in the opposite direction.

Another important factor that you will need to take into account is whether your thinking has already been shaped from a Christian standpoint, or whether you have got to work it out from scratch. You see, in theory at least, those who are outside the Christian family look at these things differently from Christians. So if you have come to faith as an adult, without the benefit of a Christian family background, you will have a new approach to financial matters to work out, and obviously, if your partner doesn't share your Christian commitment, you won't be able to do things in quite the same way as if he does.

For the sake of argument at the moment, let's assume that you are both Christians, and that you want to take God's view of money into account as you make your financial plans. This means that you will endeavour not to see your life in terms of material possessions, nor spend a high proportion of your time and energy acquiring things that you don't really need to impress people you hardly know (as can happen if we get onto the treadmill of 'keeping up with the Joneses'). Tell yourself frequently that *you* are the Joneses (to someone else!) and plan realistically to provide for your family's needs while at the same time resting in the fact that the ultimate responsibility to see that those needs are met belongs to God. When we transfer all our assets — time, money, earning power and possessions — into God's safe-keeping, it takes a great deal of the strain out of our lives.

Say what you mean

The second question that we need to answer is: 'Is what we are saying a true reflection of what we mean?' Margery and Don had many unnecessary battles over money because they tended to use 'double bind' messages in their conversations about it. Don was prone to take a very cautious view of their financial prospects, whereas Margery was generally optimistic that everything would work out all right in the end — and it had done so far (probably due to Don's foresight and planning) so why should this state of affairs not continue? Their problems were intensified because Don might declare that their chances of making ends meet that year were slim, but when Margery suggested radical measures like her returning to paid employment or selling their car and taking to bicycles, Don then insisted that they would manage somehow! This, in turn, made Margery feel that Don was painting the situation more blackly than necessary out of habit. Eventually they realised that their basic difference was one of approach. Don saw that the solution to their problems was that they should spend less, and Margery's solution was that they should earn more. When they understood this, they began to come to terms with the situation. Eventually they compromised. Margery took a part-time job, which made her feel that she was making a positive contribution to their budget, and they agreed on certain definite economies, rather than vaguely trying to 'cut down all round' as they had been doing. Their problems didn't disappear overnight; they still had a different approach to financial matters. But the important thing was that they understood each other's viewpoint and were working together instead of pulling in opposite directions.

Who does the book-keeping?

Who organises the budget and keeps the accounts in your partnership? Some couples feel that part of the husband's responsibility should be balancing the books — after all, he usually provides the greater part if not the whole of the family income. But I see nothing in the Bible to make that a scriptural principle, and if the wife is as capable or more in this area and enjoys juggling with figures, then there is no reason why she shouldn't be Chancellor, if this is the arrangement that suits them both! The vital thing is that you both agree on a budget, apportioning your money so that all the regular bills can be met, and deciding how and when anything that is left over should be spent.

Save or spend?

One man's necessity is another man's luxury as Jean and Douglas found out to their dismay, and it is in this area of non-essentials that the fights often begin. After all, if you want to keep a roof over your head, the rent or the mortgage has to be paid, but whether or not you should have a summer holiday in a tent or a guest house — or whether you should have a holiday at all, is definitely open to discussion! It takes real love and a readiness to compromise and to see the other person's viewpoint to solve these problems. It often helps to take some of the heat out of the situation if you each have some money to spend on personal items without having to account to anyone, for you may have noticed that one of the things that many wives find difficult is the thought of not having any money of their own to spend as they choose if they give up paid employment. Somehow a birthday present that is bought for your husband out of money that he has supplied for detergents or dusters lacks a certain something! So one of the options to consider is whether you should *both* have some personal spending money allocated out of the main budget. This probably won't amount to much, but having some portion of your joint income to spend exactly as you see fit, does make a difference to financial harmony, as many people who have tried it will agree.

Another thing to decide is how the budget will be administered. Will you be responsible for all the household spending while your husband deals with bills for the car, or his travel to work by other means, insurance, mortgages and so on? And what about a bank account? Will you have a joint one, on which you can both draw, or separate ones for household bills and general finances? If you haven't made use of a bank account before, do consider the possibility carefully. It really is much safer (if less satisfying) than a row of jam jars under the bed, and a monthly statement helps you to keep your affairs in order, once you have learned to figure it out!

Then there is the question of what is to be done if you find that the money won't stretch far enough and you start having niggling feelings that your partner isn't really being very careful in his spending — or he says that you are being extravagant! One way of sorting that situation out is to agree to keep a note of every penny that you spend for a week — have a small notebook kept for the purpose and take it with you everywhere. When you sit down to discuss it together you will have facts, not theories, to deal with and can see where economies might be made or where there is a genuine need for an increased allocation to that part of the budget.

Who brings home the bacon?

Gone are the days when all women equate marriage with a home-based future. Some, of course, do spend their married lives concentrating entirely on home and family, but many others want to consider full or part-time work as their children grow older and this can be a very thorny problem. Some husbands feel threatened by their wives earning a significant amount of money, and it is of little use to say they shouldn't — they do, and it is those feelings that have to be taken into account and talked through. Other men feel extremely relieved to have some of the financial burden lifted from their shoulders (and conversely, in that situation some wives feel resentful that they are expected to contribute!). So whatever category you fall into make sure that you both agree who is to provide what proportion of your income, and whether you are to make your contribution in cash or in kind!

Be a cheerful giver

One form of expenditure that a Christian should have that doesn't apply to others is tithing. Have *you* accounted for the fact that the Bibles teaches that we should give ten per cent of our income to God, as a token for everything we have comes from and belongs to him, and he has promised that if we do this he will bless us lavishly? If this is a new thought to you, you can read about it in Malachi 3.8–12. Although some Christians seem to regard this as an optional extra, a nice thing to do when they can afford it, the Bible doesn't look at it like that. In fact, it speaks of failure to give our tithes to God as being a form of robbery. Strong language! But many people who have started to tithe their income have proved the truth that God isn't any man's debtor, and if we give to him, he makes it up to us in countless, and often very practical ways.

Take Heather, for instance. Her daughter won a part-scholarship to a fee-paying school that met her academic needs in a way that her earlier school did not. Her husband Brian's income was already stretched as far as it would go so, having prayed about it, they decided that the money that Heather could earn from doing and teaching craftwork should pay the additional fees and their daughter should take up the scholarship.

All went well for the first three or four terms; Heather started to regard her craft as a job rather than a hobby and orders for her work and her sessions as a teacher provided just enough money to meet each term's bills. Then came the beginning of the new school year and a week before the due date Heather had only about half the school fee money in the bank. As she prayed about it, she was reminded that she had forgotten to tithe her craft income during that financial year. She had been so pre-occupied with making money that she had forgotten about God's share. Immediately Heather calculated what she owed and took that sum out of her craft/school fee account, leaving it even more depleted than before. But during that week, a long overdue and very hefty bill for work that she had done for a shop was paid, she sold an unusually large amount of items at a craft fair, and a complete stranger pressed an envelope into her hand after a meeting, saying that she felt God was telling her to give Heather a gift. By the end of the week, the exact amount of money that she needed for the school fees was in the bank and the bill was paid right on time.

If you haven't got round to tithing yet, why not talk about it to your partner today? You will find that it opens up a whole new area of spiritual adventure when you see God meeting your needs as he has promised. His blessings aren't reserved for the big spenders! You may not be able to give very much. This particularly applies if your husband doesn't share your Christian commitment and is not prepared to tithe your joint income. But God doesn't ask us to give what we don't have but what we do, and to do it cheerfully. Paul sums it up in his letter to the Corinthians in which he says 'If you are really eager to give, then it isn't important how much you have to give. God wants you to give what you have, not what you haven't' (1 Cor. 9.12, LB). God loves a cheerful giver, and many people over the years have discovered that when they put their financial affairs in his hands, he is a master accountant! Why not try it and see for yourself?

If money is a sensitive subject in your relationship ask yourself —

1. What is my basic attitude to money? Is it the same as my partners? If not, what can I do to improve our understanding of each other's viewpoint?

2. Are we administering our money in the best possible way? Is the one who is most capable handling it? If our affairs are in a muddle, is there someone to whom we could or should go for advice?

3. How can I demonstrate my love for my husband in material ways if this is a language of love that he understands?

   a) by being more economical?

   b) by keeping my accounts more carefully (i.e. *always* remembering to fill in my cheque stubs)?

   c) buying him some small surprise present?

   d) making a positive contribution to the family budget with a part-time/full-time job?

   e) refraining from working outside the home if that makes more economic sense at the moment and that is what he wants?

15: Body Language

'Sexual intimacy within marriage is a celebration. It is awesome, "he has taken me to his banquet hall and the banner he raises over me is love." It is satisfying, "in his longed-for shade I am seated and his fruit is sweet to my taste.' And it generates a feeling of belonging. "I am my beloved's and he is mine." ' JOYCE HUGGETT

Body language says a great deal, for it covers a very wide range of non-verbal communication. At one end of the spectrum we send messages by the way we use our hands, in gestures or touch, our eyes as we gaze lovingly into someone's face, or signal displeasure with a glare, a frown or a scowl, and with our whole bodies as we move, sit, stand or slump against a wall! The other end of the range is of course the most intimate form of sharing that there is, that of sexual intercourse. And it is in this end of the body language spectrum that many people find the greatest difficulty in expressing themselves honestly — communication on this subject is the perennial hot potato!

It is not always easy to see why this should be. There is after all no shortage of information on the subject. There are hundreds of books published on the topic of sex, and radio, TV and magazines explore every aspect that you've ever heard of (and quite a few that you haven't). In fact, it's much easier to find out about sexual matters than it is to avoid having it thrown at you at every turn.

'The way they talk about sex nowadays, you'd think someone had just invented it, and that my generation had never heard of it!' snorted one indignant grandma the other day! 'And where is all this getting them to? The divorce courts, that's where, post haste!' She may well have a point! We may find that freedom of expression is the fashion, but that very freedom has produced its own kind of bondage. Far too often sexual relationships have stopped being an expression of love and trust and oneness, and degenerated into a performance, a test we either pass or fail. We are led to believe that 'normal' couples have passionate fireworks at every encounter, and when our experience shows that sexual intimacy can also be gently satisfying, sometimes routine and occasionally elusive, we feel cheated or definitely lacking in star quality!

Now I am not suggesting that we should return to the dark ages of Victorian prudery — obviously knowledge and skill in this area is as important as in any other form of communication. In fact, almost more so, because we are so very exposed and vulnerable to criticism in something that touches the very core of our being as individuals and as a couple. But knowledge of technique is not enough. There is a person inside that body that you see as your partner and it is that person inside the body that you are making love to. So we need to set our minds not on sex, but on the person with whom we are sharing the experience; not simply on erotic expertise or getting something out of it, but on giving pleasure. Having put that attitude firmly in the forefront of our minds, we do need to face the fact that even then, things can be less than satisfactory from time to time. But they don't have to stay that way! As with all problems, if we know what is causing them, we are half way to a solution, so let's have a look at some of the reasons why we can find it difficult to say 'I love you' in Body Language!

Treat the disease, not just the symptoms!

'Would you say', asked one earnest lady at a Marriage Forum, 'that most marital problems are caused by sexual difficulties, and our inability to talk about them?'

'Not at all,' answered the doctor, who had been the main speaker. 'In fact, I would put it the other way round. Most sexual problems are merely symptoms of some other area of conflict. There are exceptions of course, but if you are having problems or advising other couples, I would suggest that you explore that avenue first. Ask yourself, "What are we really fighting about?'' because most problems have their roots outside rather than inside the bedroom door!'

That, then, is stage one! Identify the real cause of the problem and deal with that first, and you may find that you are then communicating on a physical level as never before! As Dr John Bettler rather colourfully put it, 'There isn't room in the average double bed for two grown people and two "gunny sacks". So get rid of the gunny sacks and go man, go!'

Why can't a woman be more like a man?

The flippant answer I am tempted to give to that question is 'Because it would make life very dull', but there is of course much more at stake. Don't be confused by the ardent feminists who would say 'There's no reason at all. It's all the fault of conditioning and there are no real differences other than the purely physical ones.' That suggestion comes unstuck in all manner of ways, and never more so than in the realm of our attitude and approach to sexual matters. We *are* different; we have been made differently for a purpose, and it is a difference that can heighten our enjoyment rather than detract from it, so long as we take it into account.

One of the major trouble spots in the difference between the sexes is that a man can be put into the mood for love very quickly, and predominantly through what he sees. A woman usually has a slower fuse and reacts emotionally and physically to what she feels and hears. Which is why we so often get the classic conflict situation in which a man wants to make up a quarrel by making love — the sight of his wife in a flimsy nightie can banish the memory of bitter words in an instant — whereas his wife wants the whole business sorted out first before she can contemplate a romantic finale. Neither of them are being difficult; they are just reacting true to nature. Sexual love is to him the *means* of putting things right and to her it is the *result* of putting things right. We can't alter this, so we have to learn to understand and accept it.

Look at the past as well as the present

If we want to know why someone behaves as he does today, then we need to take a careful look at yesterday. If children grow up in homes where little physical affection is demonstrated, and where sex and all things connected with it are regarded as 'not quite nice', the men and women that those children grow up to be will be likely to have the same attitude.

Simon's parents were very reserved people and what is more, his father was away a great deal. In addition to this, Simon spent his teenage years at boarding school and so, when he met and married Jo, after a whirlwind courtship, he had very little experience of normal family life to bring to their relationship. In fact he said that in all his childhood years, he could never remember seeing his parents kiss each other. Jo's upbringing had been within a very warm emotional atmosphere, and although she had always believed that intercourse belonged firmly within marriage, once that ring was on her finger she expected fireworks! So you can imagine her hurt and disappointment when, instead of being as delighted as she was in their new found freedom to express themselves, Simon froze up emotionally and felt pressurised and even threatened if she took the initiative in their love-making. Jo felt rejected, Simon felt a failure, and it looked as if their marriage was heading for the rocks before it had really set sail. Fortunately Jo was a very determined lady and she intended to make sure that her marriage would be 100% successful, not 50–50! She recognised where the real problem lay, and made a definite effort to curb her enthusiasm, while surrounding Simon with an atmosphere of warm acceptance. It took time, and eventually some professional help, but slowly and surely they have learned to meet each other's needs, and now their relationship really swings!

Chance would be a fine thing!

That is Jo and Simon's story but it is rather more commonly seen in reverse. 'Be sure to remind them,' said my husband, 'that for a man, sexual intimacy is an actual physical need, every bit as real as his need for food or sleep, especially when he is younger. The trouble is that when he wants to make love most often, his wife is usually at her most exhausted with pregnancy, babies, broken nights and toddler-filled days!' I said 'Amen' to that! And perhaps should add, 'What is more, there's no identical pattern for men or women; each individual's pattern of desire varies from person to person and within each person. But time and tiredness are two of the biggest enemies of togetherness that I know of. As Dr James Dobson says, 'By the time a mother has struggled through an eighteen hour day —especially if she has been chasing an ambitious toddler or two — her internal pilot light may have flickered and gone out. When she finally falls into bed, sex represents an obligation rather than a pleasure. . . . Meaningful sexual relations utilise great quantities of body energy and are seriously hampered when those resources have already been expended.'

Tiredness isn't just the prerogative of the young mother either. Working wives, who are in effect doing two jobs, often crawl into bed — and so do men who are giving all they've got to a demanding job. The critical difference is, though, that a man seems to find it easier to turn from being a clerk to a cavalier at the flick of a switch, than his wife does from being 'Mom' one minute to 'Madame' the next! So what can we do about it?

1. Recognise that this area of communication is very important, and if it is important to make time to talk, it is equally important to make time to love. Both are vital forms of communication and of course, when one is working well, the other is usually given a boost.

2. Make guarding against over-tiredness a priority. Now, if you are snorting at that suggestion, I'm snorting with you! I *know* how difficult it is. For some reason, we feel guilty about putting our feet up for half an hour in order to feel rested later in the day, and yet why should we? We don't feel like that about preparing ahead to entertain friends, or getting certain jobs done in advance so that we can go out unhindered. So why can't we accept that preserving some energy for 'us' is an equally worth-

while motive? And if we can get away from home occasionally, even if it is only for a night, let's grab the chance. That feeling of relaxation and 'being away from it all' does wonders for our awareness of each other, and there is no need to feel guilty. As one husband said when his wife queried whether they could afford the trip, 'Dare we not afford it? Is there anything that we can spend money on that is more important than strengthening our marriage?'

Swings and roundabouts

It must be very difficult for men to understand the monthly mood swings that women have to cope with. After all, if you have never woken up with a backache, stomach cramps, a feeling that you are the ugliest woman that you have ever seen and an overwhelming desire to snap at everyone you meet, it must be difficult to imagine what it feels like!

Of course, not every woman suffers like that all of the time, but pre-menstrual tension is a fact of life, not a figment of our imagination. Did you know that, according to one study of the problem, 63% of English women were in the pre-menstrual period when they had accidents, committed crimes or committed suicide? So, if your husband isn't in the know about these things, pass the word on! But a rather lesser known fact is that men, too, have mood swings over a period of time which can be charted, so we shouldn't expect to have all the sympathy — understanding and sensitivity are needed on both sides.

You may find it helpful to talk about the occasions when you notice that a 'bout of the blues' is likely to occur to one or the another. Do a bit of detective work and make a note in the diary or calender, so that you can be prepared — and keep off touchy subjects for those few days. And remember, it's no use saying, 'You shouldn't feel like that' If your partner *does* feel like it that won't help. Sometimes there are positive things we can do, pressures that we can relieve; at other times we just have to ride out the storm. No one can expect to be 'up' all the time, nor should we demand it from each other. Instead, let's accept that a changing pattern of emotions is inevitable, and give light and shade to our lives together. We can offer love and support without going to the extreme of encouraging our partner to wallow in depression or self-pity.

Mind your motives

The Bible teaches that sexual love is God's gift to us, and we are not only free to enjoy it within marriage, but actually encouraged to do so. It is part of the marital package deal and we are not to short-change each other! In sexual communication we demonstrate our love and acceptance of our partner, and we both give and get happiness, satisfaction and a sense of belonging, to mention just some of the benefits. But sometimes things go wrong because we twist this form of communication to —

1. Repay a real or imagined debt or secure a favour.
2. Try to gain attention or overcome a sense of inferiority.
3. Use it to manipulate our partner by supplying or withholding sexual intimacy as a punishment or reward.

Verity and Phil had a problem. Phil had a very demanding job in the police force and his hours were irregular to say the least. Verity felt that he could get home earlier if he tried, and one night decided to greet him with the 'glamour routine' in an effort to encourage him into better habits. Consequently, she donned her most alluring housecoat, quantities of perfume and had a candle-lit supper on a tray ready when he came in. You can imagine her fury when he followed his usual custom of eating and then falling asleep in front of the television! 'He didn't even notice!' she complained bitterly the next day. But she was wrong there. Phil had noticed. But he had also noticed that her attitude didn't match her outfit. Verity was trying to manipulate him and he resisted her all down the line. And it wasn't until she decided that she would be loving and available to him with no strings attached, that his working day mysteriously became shorter!

Don't try to read his mind

There are times when non-verbal communication is very effective, but difficulties are best sorted out with words. And this is where many of us grind to a halt. We find it incredibly difficult to put our needs into words and are afraid of making a delicate situation worse with some ill-chosen gaffe. But we *can* learn to express ourselves in this area and much of what we have considered already will help us.

1. *Choose the right time and place* Many people find it easier to talk with the lights out, and if the experience of love-making that you have just enjoyed has been a happy and satisfactory one, then 'pillow-talk' has a lot to recommend it — sharing while you are still feeling happy and relaxed. But if you are tense and unhappy, then dark or not, you may find it better to wait for another occasion.

2. *Choose the right words* Remember 'I' messages; they avoid anything you say sounding like an accusation. 'I want to make you happy . . .', 'What can I do to . . .?' 'I like it when you . . .'

3. *Remember* that if you are fearful he is probably just as ill at ease. So don't be threatening — 'I think we're hopeless' or 'So-and-so always does . . .' — but positive — 'How can we do better?'

4. *Express appreciation*, affection and admiration. The bedroom is not the place to criticise.

5. *If you are really stuck*, try writing down a sentence or two about how you feel in those notebooks we mentioned earlier, and then exchanging them. It often only needs a small chink in the dam to let the waters start flowing; you may like to try some of these questions for a start —

   a) Did I bring any sexual hang-ups that I am aware of to our marriage? Have I ever shared them with my partner?

   b) If we are having problems in this area, are there any obvious underlying causes? What am I prepared to do about them?

   c) Are our natural differences in approach causing difficulties, or have we learned to deal with them, and even make use of them?

d) How are we doing in the 'time and tiredness' stakes? What definite steps are we taking to make time for relaxed enjoyment of each other?

e) Am I giving and receiving sexual pleasure in the way that God intended, or am I using it as a weapon to manipulate and manoeuvre my partner?

f) What are we doing to improve this aspect of our communication and to make it fun?

16: Family Matters

'In raising children, all you can do is your best. If your child ultimately grows up to honour God, consider it a miracle. We can do the possible but we can't do miracles. So we take care of the possible and leave the impossible to God.' RUTH GRAHAM

In a recent radio programme on family life, two well-known ladies were quoted as having had a rather dramatic change of viewpoint. Betty Friedan and Erin Pizzey, two of the leading champions of women's rights both agreed that the Women's Liberation movement has failed to a significant extent. And it has failed in their opinion because the people in it have concentrated on external things — equal rights, equal opportunities, easy access to contraception and abortion and so on, instead of trying to find better ways for men and women to live together and bring up their children. According to Ms Pizzey, 'The happiest family is one that is open to the community and involved in and committed to it.'

I would agree with Ms Friedan and Pizzey that the Women's Liberation Movement has made quite a few mistakes. But my recipe for family happiness would be somewhat different. Although I wouldn't dare to claim to have discovered the perfect mixture, I would suggest that the happiest families are —

— committed to each other, to the world around them and to God,
— caring for each other, for the world around them and for God,
— communicating with each other, the world around them and with God.
— challenged to discover and achieve their full potential.

That's quite a target, isn't it? And goals like that are easily written down but not so easily accomplished! You may well ask, 'How can we start to bring about this desirable state of affairs?'

Starting at square one, we need to grasp that a family may be many things, but there is one thing that it is not and never will be — a perfect group of flawless people! And one of the many areas in which we will try, struggle, and fail, and pick ourselves up to try again, is the area of communication! You may be heard to mutter, 'Mother, is it worth it?' but persevere! For if you can communicate with your *own* children and relations, you'll probably find that you can do the same with *anyone's* child or relations, and many of these principles can be applied to any group, whether it is a Sunday School class, youth club, or simply the people next door.

Know their needs

Dr Mia Kelmer Pringle, who has made a detailed study of the emotional needs of children (which, incidentally, tally pretty closely with the emotional needs of the rest of us!) says that there are four basic things that we have to communicate to them in words, attitudes and actions.

First, children need to know love and the security which comes from consistent loving care by one person. They need to hear us say, verbally and non-verbally, 'You're accepted; you belong; *you* are someone special!'

Secondly, they used praise and recognition for their achievements, however small. This gives them a healthy sense of significance, and of being worth something — self image again! In Dr Pringle's view, a child's attitude to himself and to learning will decide how effectively he learns, just as much as, if not more than, his actual abilities. And we contribute to that self-image by our praise and recognition!

The third thing that is important to a child is to have opportunities for growth and development through new experiences, in the company of those he loves and trusts, and through play. Notice that here again, our participation is important. We provide the opportunities, the tools and the scope for exploration and adventure.

Finally, a child needs to achieve, and this need is met by the way in which he is allowed to become increasingly responsible for his own actions and decisions. Responsibility is a skill and, like all other skills, it needs to be practised.

Set the scene

It isn't enough to know what we need to communicate, it is also necessary to create the kind of atmosphere in which communication is not only possible but positive and healthy.

If you had a barometer which could register emotional rather than air pressure in your home, how would it read today? Stormy? Heavy and sultry? Very cold? If you have never thought about it, do stop and give it some consideration now, because the emotional climate in a family has a direct bearing on the communication patterns. Angry parents very often produce angry children! Of course it isn't 100% up to the parents; children, especially older ones, have a very definite contribution to make. But your attitude and actions in four key areas will go a long way to create an atmosphere in which your child's needs for acceptance, significance, growth, development and achievement can be met. Give priority to:

1. LOVE AND DISCIPLINE

The apostle John reminds us that there is no fear in love (1 Jn 4.18) and since fear is one of the greatest barriers to open sharing, it follows that where there is a plentiful supply of love, fear will be kept to a minimum and barriers laid low. Love opens the door to disciplined freedom, but notice that this doesn't mean that individuals do their own thing regardless of others. Discipline is the balancing factor; discipline that is fair, firm, and, above all, consistent. As one headmistress put it, 'Children need absolute freedom within rigidly defined limits.' When they have this they feel secure.

2. AUTHORITY AND TRUST

In this anti-authoritarian age, authority is almost a dirty word. But if a child is ever going to become self-disciplined, he has first to accept discipline and respect authority, and, for a young child, authority *is* his parents! Now that does *not* mean that we have to rule with an iron rod, with no consideration of the feelings and wishes of the rest of the family, but a young child does have to learn to accept the authority of his parents and to know that there are times when that authority had to be submitted to without explanation. After all, if my small son is about to cycle into the road in front of a car and I shout 'Stop', his very life will depend on his obedience. With his older brothers and sisters there is a greater emphasis on trust — on both sides — but for trust to develop, parents have to show themselves to be trustworthy. Can your child say with assurance 'My parents always mean what they say; I can rely on their word absolutely'? Remember, unpredictable parents threaten their children's security!

3. ENCOURAGEMENT AND OPENNESS

What is the ratio of criticism to compliments in your family? If you had a tape recording of today's conversations, would it show anything like the desirable norm of 80%

compliments to 20% criticism? For most of us, most of the time, the sad answer would have to be 'no', even though we all thrive on encouragement. There are so many small misdemeanours that would be far better ignored, for if we constantly criticise, it becomes destructive, the person we are criticising tends to 'tune out' and ceases to hear us.

Annette was having a constant battle with her son over his table manners. Every meal time she corrected him, and every meal time he repeated the errors until their time at the table turned into a battle-ground and life was made miserable for the entire family. Eventually, Annette had an idea. Taking her son on one side she said, 'If you will make an effort to behave properly at meal times for two weeks, I promise that I will stop correcting you for that time.' In addition to that spoken bargain she made an unspoken promise to herself to compliment Alan as often as she could, and the transformation to the emotional climate was amazing. For by the end of two weeks, both Annette and Alan had developed some good habits, broken some bad ones, and reached a new understanding of each other!

4. FREEDOM FOR GROWTH

'As it was in the beginning, is now, and ever shall be . . .' Continuity and regularity are two important factors in creating the secure background that children need, but taken to extremes, they can become stultifying and deadening. What is the growth factor in your family (I'm thinking now in terms of minds rather than bodies)? Do you greet any suggestion for doing something new with an 'Oh; but . . .!' or a 'How could we fit it in?' If it doesn't work out quite according to plan, never mind. You will all learn something from the experience, so be open to change, for as my father so often says, 'The man who never made a mistake, never made anything.'

Check your attitude!

As we have already seen, criticism can have a deadly and counter productive effect, but all these outward reactions stem from an inner attitude. If I regard my children as a nuisance and rate them low on my order of priorities, they will notice that I am always too busy to listen to them, or, if I do listen, that I am only giving them half my attention. If I think that children can't be expected to be sensible and responsible, I will be reluctant to let them try anything new or slightly difficult. If I see my child as an extension of myself instead of an individual in his own right, I will feel overly responsible for his success or failure or let down by his misbehaviour. I may not say any of these things in words, but children will sense the attitude behind the action.

Make sharing times fun

What are your priorities? Can you think of an occasion in this past week when you have deliberately put time on one side to spend relating to, and communicating with, each of your children? Do you look for things you can do together that genuinely interest you both? Cricket and board war games have been marvellous shared interests for my husband and sons and have kept communication flowing in two areas at least when other things have been hard going. And we have tried to make a rule that the television is never used as a background — if there is nothing on that we really want to watch, the 'off' switch is brought into operation, and we do something else — together, at least occasionally.

Learn to listen with your eyes

I can usually tell by the way my children come through the kitchen door in the evening what kind of a day they have had. 'Hello, Mom, I'm home!' can be said in a dozen different ways, and a glance at their faces, the set of their shoulders, and the speed of their steps, can quickly suggest to me whether I should offer tea and sympathy, words of encouragement, or accept their 'not bad', as I enquire about their day, at face value, and let both of us go straight about our business.

Treat 'em right!

In a group discussion the members of the group were asked to think about how they could apply Paul's injunction to 'be kind to one another' in their own homes. After a few minutes' thought, one woman said, 'I'm going to treat my own family with the same consideration as I show to visitors,' and she got a round of applause!

Are you a double standard family where 'anything goes' for us, but for strangers it's a different matter? I've always been aware of this danger and have actively tried to avoid it, but I don't think I can have succeeded too well. A few years ago we had two small friends to stay for the first week of the summer holidays, and it just so happened that there was a great deal on that week to which I had already planned to take my three children. After a week of visits to the cinema, the East of England show, picnics, swimming and a trip on the river, we saw our visitors off at the station. As we left the platform our second son looked at me and beamed. 'We've had a lovely time with Johnny and Philip, haven't we?' he said, and then stopped. 'Did we do it because you wanted to or were you just trying to make a good impression?'

Well, there you have it! We can do our best and still be misunderstood. But if we are aware of our children's needs, create the right atmosphere and are ready to make use of the opportunities for family sharing, we will be prepared when the occasion arises to communicate emotionally, in practical ways and through our words, with the tinies, the teenagers and all the stages in between.

17: The Growing Years

'What you say and forget today, a child may carry inside him for the rest of his life.'

Communication starts in the cradle! Just because a baby can't talk doesn't mean that it can't communicate. In fact, before a baby can say a word it communicates distress by crying and body movements (from birth), responds to its parents' presence and voice by gurgling and smiling —communicating pleasure (from 4–8 weeks) — and begins to babble and experiment with sound and intonation (from 4–8 months). So it is never too soon to start talking to our children, and to realise that we are communicating by the way we hold them, by the tone of our voice as we speak to them and by the atmosphere that surrounds them, from the moment of birth.

Have you seen the world from your child's level just recently? If you have small children, try walking round on your knees for a few minutes! What do you see? The table isn't a flat surface on which to put things but a roof over your head. The dog seems bigger, the cupboards taller, the windows give you just a glimpse of the world outside! And as we try to communicate with our young children, we need to bear this constantly in mind. A small child does see the world as a different place, in terms of size and in terms of meaning, because he hasn't yet had enough experience to interpret it as you do. He also gets different information from the words he hears, for some he only half understands, others are so similar in sound that he can easily confuse one with another.

Claire was watching television with her two small sons, aged four and six, and, during the course of the programme, the subject of the misuse of drugs was mentioned. In response to their questions, Claire took the opportunity to explain to the boys how dangerous drugs could be, and how carefully they needed to be handled. A day or two later she noticed that her elder son, Peter, was very quiet and obviously had something on his mind. For a couple of days he remained withdrawn and she couldn't get to the bottom of the problem until, at bedtime, gentle probing brought it all tumbling out.

'Mummy,' sobbed Peter, 'I've taken drugs.'

'Really darling, when?' queried Claire, wondering what on earth he meant.

'We have them every day at school,' he replied tearfully. 'They're in the bottom of our cocoa cups.'

For a moment Claire was still mystified. Visions of a juvenile Mafia flashed into her mind. And then she realised what Peter meant. He was referring to the *dregs* of his drink — a simple mistake, but one that had given him two fear-filled days!

Peter's problem arose, partly because he had a wide vocabulary — many six year olds would have described the deposit from the cocoa grounds as 'bits', and the misunderstanding would not have happened. But how can we help our children if they are not fluent talkers in their pre-school days, either because they are naturally quiet and shy, or because they are slow developers in this area? In our family we have had to work this problem out because, when our small foster daughter came to live with us at four years old, she was very hard to understand, and found it equally hard to express herself. Her brother, 15 months older, spoke clearly when he spoke at all, but if you asked him to explain anything, he was floundering within seconds. It must have been quite a shock to them to be pitch-forked into a family which is rarely at a loss for words! It was certainly back to the books and the experts for me, to try and find out how to help, and these are some of the suggestions which I had offered to me.

Give them a chance to speak

There is a danger of parents anticipating their children's needs and being too impatient to listen to their stumbling and faltering efforts to express them. But that is counter-productive. If you remove the need for making an effort, they will cease to make it — that's perfectly natural! So wait, and let them get it out, and discourage older brothers and sisters from interpreting too freely!

In a large or noisy family there is sometimes a need for parents to impose a 'turn' system — 'Angus is speaking now, then we'll hear what David wants to say, and then it is Robert's turn' — in order to prevent meal-times from sounding like a football match with each one yelling above the others in order to make himself heard. You may have noticed that I said 'he'. In our family the boys do tend to dominate the conversation unless checked, and it has drawn our attention to the need to give individual attention to each one, and particularly to the quieter ones, if meaningful communication is to take place. Our daughters chatter non-stop if their brothers are out of the way, and so it is up to us, as parents, to make sure that opportunities are made for this to happen.

Encourage their efforts

No child is going to use perfect grammar when he is learning to speak (do we?) and the important thing is to accept and encourage him in his efforts to communicate rather than constantly correcting what is, at the moment, beyond his understanding. If we respond in our normal speech, without excessive correction or explanation, he will soon learn the correct sentence structure and an adequate vocabulary. Occasionally, of course, it is necessary to try and straighten things out, but if this happens, try saying 'If you said . . . I would understand you better,' rather than 'Don't say . . . say . . .!' Remember that children learn by imitation — which causes me to ask myself at frequent intervals 'What are my children seeing and hearing to imitate?' 'Don't do as I do, do as I say' might have worked in the Victorian era, but it certainly doesn't cut much ice in the last quarter of the twentieth century. As I have already mentioned, Robert has a limited vocabulary, but it is expanding, and one of his favourite words is 'hypocrite'! He knows what *that* means and he flings it around with deadly accuracy!

Stimulate your children to ask questions!

Some parents may feel that that statement is way off beam —their small children never stop! The most oft-repeated word in many a household is that awful question 'Why?' and some of us feel that we shall scream if we hear it once more in a day! Perhaps the heading might seem better phrased if it suggested that we should 'stimulate parents to answer questions and answer them truthfully'! Well, of course, both parts are necessary. Children do ask questions, and often, at certain stages ask them incessantly, but we do need to be aware that there are some areas about which they may not put their questions into words (sexual matters is one of these with some children) and be ready to stimulate questions and fill in the gaps where required.

And answers are important too! It is particularly important that we should reply to questions immediately they arise if possible, or as soon as is feasible afterwards. If we genuinely don't know the answer to their query, then we should say so, and set plans afoot for discovering what it is together. What we must *not* do is to offer a half-truthful explanation for the sake of simplicity, which we will have to un-say later. Sometimes we have to say, 'Wait, and you will understand more later' and that *can* be a perfectly valid answer in some circumstances. When our second son was four, he fixed me with a stern gaze after we had said prayers one evening and said, 'You tell me all this about God, but how do I know that you're right? Perhaps one of the false gods is really the right one to believe in!' How would you have dealt with that one? Somewhat taken aback, I pointed him to creation and Jesus (in very simple terms) but eventually I had to say, 'When you are older you will learn more about these things and be able to decide for yourself what is right', and with that he was satisfied — for a little while!

Help them to distinguish between fantasy and reality

This can be very difficult. When small children have a vivid imagination it can be a hard job to sort out truth from fiction because to them, the dividing line is so thin as to be non-existent. When Angus was little he was terrified of some imaginary horrors called 'Town Creatures' which haunted his dreams and had a nasty habit of hiding under beds and in cupboards! He could not describe them to us but they were very real to him and it was no good accusing him of lying or trying to argue them away. On the other hand it was not very sensible to agree that we could see them too, and frighten him still further! Listening over and over again, talking about the difference between the things we could see with our mind's eye and the things we could see with our physical eyes, and claiming the presence and protection of an all powerful and ever loving Lord Jesus, banished the Town Creatures eventually, but it took some doing!

Read to your child

If you are a 'bookish' family, this may seem an unnecessary suggestion, but many many families (somewhere in the region of 70%) own less than 5 books. Yes, I know there are public libraries, but it makes you wonder how many children are read to regularly. And yet, reading to your child is an excellent base for communication; you share pleasure, you share physical contact as you sit snuggled up together and you share knowledge that you can talk about afterwards. But there is an additional bonus. If part of that reading is of Bible stories or of the Bible itself, the door is then open for the natural sharing discussion of spiritual truths. Remember the slogan, 'an apple a day keeps the doctor away'! Well, perhaps we should devise a new one for family sharing which would say, 'a story at night keeps communication right'!

Keep an eye on the TV

There is no doubt that television is not only here to stay but is going to be available to us for a larger and larger proportion of the day. And so the temptation to use it as an electronic babysitter, or to allow it to kill family conversations stone dead as meals are eaten in front of it, will become more and more pressing. But television can be a stimulus to sharing and conversation instead of a communication killer, if we will observe at least some of the following guide-lines —

1. Have a set that can be moved around, and if it is at all possible, keep it out of the main living area for at least some of the time.

2. Invest in the television programme magazines and encourage children to choose their programmes in advance, within agreed limits on type, timing and number of programmes viewed. Discuss with them what kind of programmes fall within the 'acceptable' category for your family and why — it helps them to be selective. Children can be amazingly reasonable if we explain things in terms that they can understand.

3. If you make a rule like 'no television before homework or after 7.00 pm on school days', stick to it!

4. Limit meals eaten in front of the television to an occasional treat (we have Saturday evening supper on our laps, and apart from occasional sporting events, that's it).

5. If you are unsure of the suitability of a programme, watch it with them, warn them beforehand that you will use the 'off' switch if necessary, and do it!

6. Take the opportunities for discussion raised by the programmes. Encourage critical appraisal of the advertisements especially, and help them to see the manipulative techniques of the advertisers and the false view of life that they so often present.

7. Enjoy the good programmes together! Friends of ours used to watch the Friday evening western as a family. They had 'Cowboy Chow' (sausages and beans for supper), the boys had their six-shooters at the ready to join in with the gunfights, and everyone had a great time. That may not be your idea of an evening's entertainment, but there are plenty of good programmes to suit most tastes, and we need to teach the children (and ourselves) how to get the best out of this marvel of science, as well as being aware of its dangers.

Remember communication is not all words

One of the earliest forms of communication that most babies experience is being cradled in their mother's arms, and touch continues to be a vital form of communication throughout life. We are *never* too old for a cuddle or a hug, and it can sometimes get through to people when everything else has failed.

Georgina and Colin decided that it was right to add to their family, but since they already had two children of their own, they wanted to share their family life and love with a child who might otherwise never know anything but institutional care. After many delays and disappointments Tamarisk came into their lives, a mixed-race war orphan from Cambodia, who had spent the first five years of her life in an orphanage in her own country, and another two or three in an English institution. She was slightly mentally and physically retarded, but her biggest handicap was emotional. Tamarisk had tantrums! She had them whenever she couldn't do anything, and as that happened several times each day and night at first, Georgina's wisdom and patience was stretched to the limit. She tried everything — talking, demonstrating and disciplining, but the only thing that had any effect was 'hug-therapy', as the family called it. Whenever Tamarisk flung herself down on the floor in a fury of screams and tears, Georgina (or Colin if he was at home) picked her up — or lay on the floor too, if she was kicking too hard — and cuddled her. Tamarisk didn't seem very appreciative at first, but gradually her new parents noticed that although she was kicking and biting and apparently trying to escape the encircling arms, she was also hanging on for all that she was worth to make sure that they did not let her go. It was an uphill struggle, but eventually the tantrums lessened, and Tamarisk began to return their love. Communication became two-way, in words as well as in actions, although for her, even now, touch says more than anything else.

Keep your goal in view

Communication is not an end in itself, but a process for getting your message through. For that reason it is very important not to lose sight of what the message is in the midst of all the 'how to's' of getting it across. So ask yourself frequently, 'What, in the final analysis, are we trying to communicate to our children? What are our goals for our family life together? Is our main purpose that they should "turn out all right" — whatever that means to us — and be a satisfactory product of our good parenting? Or is our ground plan to provide opportunities for each one to reach their full potential, to be committed to, communicating with and caring for, each other, the world around them and their God?'

Remember that we cannot force our children to go in any one direction. As Ruth Graham says, we have to 'take care of the possible, and leave the impossible up to God'. This is true right from the beginning of family life, but never more so than when it comes to living with and communicating to teenagers.

18: The Testing Years

'Adolescence is a period of temporary insanity, but take courage — this too will pass.'

'Before I got married, I had six theories about bringing up children; now I have six children and no theories!' That penetrating statement was made by John Wilmot, Earl of Rochester, and believe it or not, he lived three hundred years ago! Which goes to show that human nature doesn't change much — I could have written the very same thing myself (except that I had rather more theories and have one less child).

One of the areas in which theories abound is the handling and problems of teenagers. When our children were small I started to read a book on the subject and felt so depressed after a few pages that I tossed the book away, with a vague hope that the Second Coming would occur before our trio reached that dreaded age! Well, it hasn't and they have, and I have come to the conclusion that one of the problems with teenagers is that they have a very bad Press image! We somehow expect them to change overnight when they reach that ominous milestone of thirteen, and either expect the worst (and are therefore likely to predispose it to happen) or demand too much and are then disappointed at how far below our standards of adult behaviour they fall!

Let's be realistic in our hopes and fears for this stage of family life. Yes, it can be difficult, as both parents and children have to adjust to each other's needs and, by trial and error, have to work out new patterns of freedom and responsibility. Yes, teenagers are noisy, demanding, moody, inconsiderate and inconsistent sometimes! But they can also be thoughtful, supportive, helpful, entertaining, refreshing, clear-sighted and fun! And it is possible to keep the doorway to communication open if we will remember two things.

First of all, we should not expect them to be spiritual or emotional giants — giants are freaks. We must let them be what they are — developing individuals who are falling down, getting up again, learning lessons and growing in fits and starts. Secondly, although the principles of family living and loving stay the same — they still need love, security, a measure of discipline, a chance to develop and achieve, and plenty of praise and recognition — the ways in which these principles will be worked out will change, perhaps more than once, in the course of the teenage years. And this is where we as parents, need to be flexible and clear-sighted.

Carry on talking

If you have established good patterns of communication from earliest childhood, then you have a sound basis on which to build in later years. But supposing you have not done too well so far, and have reached the teenage stage with your family sharing still a very patchy affair — what can you do to improve matters?

a) Take a survey!

Tape-record your evening meal-time conversation from Monday to Friday without drawing attention to the fact, then play it back with a pencil and paper in your hand. Ask some or all of the family to listen to it with you (most of us love to hear ourselves on tape) and to make a note of the answers to the following questions:

1. What are the main topics of conversation and who brings them up?
2. Who talks the most? (You might have to take a vote on that!)
3. What topics of conversation do you avoid as a family?
4. Who talks most about feelings?
5. Who talks most about facts?
6. Who doesn't talk at all unless directly addressed?
7. What proportion of compliments to criticism is handed out and by whom?

This will give you a pretty clear picture of the situation as it is, and with older children it is possible to say, 'Look, this shows that we are doing too much arguing/gossiping/criticising, etc. — let's see if we can make meal-times more pleasant by banning fights, and making sure that everyone gets an opportunity to say what is on his/her mind without interruption'. You may find that the next meal is eaten in total silence, but after that, things can improve if you will give a positive lead and, like the hostess at a formal dinner party, keep the conversational ball rolling along in the right direction.

b) Make the time

'It's no use suggesting that we should communicate at meal-times,' said Louise wearily, 'we just never sit down together. Breakfast is a running buffet, with the emphasis on the "running", and in the evening we all come in (and go out) at different times.' Is that the situation you face? If so, there are various possible solutions. In most families it is possible to make one meal in the week a 'sit-down-to-gether' do, either on a week-night or at a week-end. And if you can't all be together, there is a plus factor in having one or two members of the family on their own to talk to on a one to one basis.

Meals are not the only time for talking either. I remember one friend with a large and widely spaced family saying that she was weary because she was up early in the morning with her toddler, and had to stay awake late at night to listen to her teenagers. I was surprised at the time, but now I know what she meant. It is amazing what interesting facts and passionately held beliefs are expounded from the foot of one's bed late at night!

Polly found this bed-time chat to be the saving of her relationship with her eldest son. Seventeen-year-old Nicholas was the most difficult, as well as the oldest of her five children, and friction in the household reached flash-point just two days after her husband, who was in the Navy, set off on a nine month voyage. Nick was packed and ready to leave home when the phone rang to say that a close relation had been killed in a road accident. The shock sobered the whole family, and it wasn't until after the funeral that the subject of his future was discussed again.

'I don't really want to move out,' he told his mother, 'but I know that we can't go on like this. If I stay, can I have the time that you and Dad usually spend reading and praying together with you, and make sure that the others know that they can't muscle in?' Gladly Polly agreed, and for nine months, that half hour at the end of the day was reserved exclusively for Nick. Sometimes they just chatted about the needs of the family or the events of the day. Occasionally they read the Bible or prayed together over some particular problem, at other times they just listened to the news. You might say that the communication wasn't very profound, but it happened and it happened regularly. Polly is sure that it was principally this time together which transformed their relationship, and when Nick did leave home twelve months later, to go into the Navy himself, there was heartache of the right sort at their parting!

It may not always be very convenient to make yourself available when your children want you, but it is so important. Pat worked from home, and as she had school age children, the hours when they were out of the house were her working time and very precious. But one of her older sons, Paul, who had moved into a flat nearby and worked a night shift took to calling in for breakfast after work and spending up to a couple of hours chatting to her in the kitchen. Her schedule was seriously disrupted by this, and several times she almost told him that she must get on with some work, but some inner prompting restrained her. How glad she was that she had listened to the Holy Spirit's gentle voice when Paul was killed in a tragic accident just a few months later. 'Those hours in the kitchen when he shared so many of his hopes, his fears and his dreams are among my most precious memories,' she said. 'We so often put off our attempts at communication until a more convenient time, but we need to take what today has to offer. Tomorrow may never come.'

c) Say what needs to be said

As children grow older we have to slacken the reins by degrees and allow them more and more freedom to make their own decisions and be responsible for their own actions. But there are times when even fifteen or sixteen year-olds are secretly glad to have parental prohibitions to protect them from the pressures of their group, and in our anxiety to avoid rows and confrontations, we have to chart that complicated course between being spineless and being sensible. Yes, teenagers do want privacy, and are not always anxious or even willing to discuss their problems with their parents. Yes, we do have to accept that suggestions which would be spurned if they came from our lips may be hailed as pearls of wisdom when they come from someone else. But we do have a responsibility to see that they are adequately informed about such matters as smoking, drugs, alcohol, sex, the occult and their spiritual position before God, and not to assume that they will have learned all they need to know from school, the church or some other source. And we also need to remember that we will be expected to live by the standards that we hold up as desirable for them. All children notice inconsistency in their parents to a greater or lesser degree, but there is no keener or more critical judge of parental behaviour than a teenage son or daughter. Anything we say is certain to be remembered and any deviation from it will surely be noted down and used in evidence against us!

Don't be afraid of feelings

When you think about it, a household containing parents in middle life and teenage children is an emotional powder keg. Mother may be approaching the menopause and having to deal with various negative emotions brought on by the thought of her soon-departing brood, and what she may see as her own potential redundancy. Father is probably at the most pressurised time of his job or career, perhaps keeping an eye on those climbing the ladder beneath him or facing the limitations of his own ambitions and achievements. And then there are the children battling with hormonal changes, peer pressures, the stress of exams and job hunting, and the urge for independence and freedom! Whew! It's only by the grace of God that there aren't more problems than there are!

Teaching children to handle their emotions is a whole new subject in itself which space will not allow us to explore in detail in this book. But in communicational terms we can perhaps note two things —

1. Christians are not immune from the problems and pressures of life, quite the reverse, and parents who try to persuade their children that the Christian life will be joy all the time are doing them a great disservice. For this

reason when we have difficulties we might do well to admit it, for emotions that are bottled up erupt sooner or later. So as a family, let's encourage one another to be open about how we feel and, without venting our frustrations or negative emotions on other-people unnecessarily, allow those we love to share the downs as well as the ups. After all, the Bible tells us to 'be happy with those who are happy' and to 'weep with those who weep' (Rom. 12.15, GNB). Sometimes I find it useful to alert the other members of the family when one or another is feeling out of sorts. A private word of warning about teasing or provocative remarks or a request for temporary kid-glove handling can often prevent friction. And prayer for and about each other's needs is a wonderful resource always available.

2. Not letting the sun go down on your anger applies to children too. It isn't easy to say sorry, but resentments and injustices (real or imaginary) can fester and pollute relationships if left. Are you willing to make the first move? Taking the initiative in restoring relationships and reinstating communication may not be any easier for you or me than it is for our children, but we have the greater responsibility to see that it is done. And if we can teach our children how to handle conflict constructively, to listen reflectively, and to explain their feelings without accusing others, we shall have made a very important contribution to their future happiness.

Have we no rights?

When I asked my children what, in their estimation, the most important problem factor in communication between parents and teenage children is, the flippant reply was that parents are born thirty years too early and don't 'freak the scene'! That last phrase, translated into normal English, means that parents don't always understand the culture of the day as their children see it, and that is hardly surprising when we realise that the youth culture is changing so completely as to be almost unrecognisable, about every five years! The other problem as they saw it, was a lack of willingness to compromise from both parties, but particularly on the teenager's side! Well, it's refreshing to think that they might be in the wrong sometimes!

An awareness of life as it is for each family member *now*, and a willingness to compromise, *are* two of the most important factors in good communication at any time. We need to make an effort to understand, and we also need to be understood. But there are other needs which both parents and children have the right to expect to be met within the family circle, and these too will improve the level and content of our sharing together. Talk about these things together and see if you agree with me that:

1. PARENTS AND CHILDREN HAVE THE RIGHT TO BE THEMSELVES

We often bend over backwards to accept our children as they are. Will they accord us the same privilege — accepting our right to our own point of view, interests, likes and dislikes — even if these are twenty years behind the times in some cases?

2. PARENTS AND CHILDREN HAVE THE RIGHT TO BE HONEST

'Speaking the truth in love' is an option that should be equally available to all!

3. PARENTS AND CHILDREN HAVE A RIGHT TO ASK QUESTIONS AND TO BE GIVEN HONEST ANSWERS

Sometimes that honest answer might be 'don't know' or 'that is a personal matter that I don't feel free to discuss with you just now' and that too must be respected.

4. PARENTS AND CHILDREN HAVE THE RIGHT TO THINK THEIR OWN THOUGHTS AND BELIEVE THEIR OWN BELIEFS

It is very easy, isn't it, in the heat of the discussion to say, 'you shouldn't think/believe/feel that way'? We all need a degree of freedom and privacy, and that applies to the mind as well as the body.

5. PARENTS AND CHILDREN HAVE THE RIGHT TO MAKE DECISIONS AND TO CONTRIBUTE TO ANY DECISION THAT WILL AFFECT THEM

Family forums are exhausting but important. Teenage children do have a right to make their point of view known about such things as holidays, major changes in family routine and life-style and so on, but once again this works both ways. My children may decide that they will go to a concert fifty miles away, but that does not oblige me to decide that I will drive them there and back! I have a right to be consulted and to make my own decision!

6. PARENTS AND CHILDREN HAVE THE RIGHT TO GROW AND DEVELOP AT THEIR OWN PACE

We are all growing, developing and changing, and children contribute just as much to their parents' spiritual and emotional growth as we do to theirs. When they drive us to our knees in desperate prayer, dispute our ideas about life and challenge our acceptance of the status quo, they keep us from sinking into comfortable complacency. But they must allow us to grow at our own pace, just as we must do the same for them. And then perhaps we will discover one day, rather to our surprise, that we are all a little wiser, a little more mature, a lot more loving. In other words, that we *have* come a long way towards being committed to, caring for, and communicating with each other, the world around us and with God.

19: Hot-line to Heaven

> '*Happy are the couples who do recognise and understand that their happiness is a gift of God, who can kneel together to express their thanks, not only for the love which he has put into their hearts, the children he has given them or all of life's joys, but also for the progress in their marriage which he brings about through that hard school of mutual understanding.*' PAUL TOURNIER

Couples who share a living commitment to a common Christian faith are privileged people. But they are also in peril if they assume that simply because they are Christians, their relationship will automatically run smoothly. Certainly God is the designer of marriage and as such, he can give us the wisdom and insight to make it work. But marriages that are made in heaven still have to be lived out on earth, and we need to come to him on a regular basis for that help, love and understanding which will keep our relationship on the right course. Jesus put it in a nutshell when he said to his disciples 'Remain united to me, and I will remain united to you . . . for you can do nothing without me' (Jn. 15.4, 5, GNB).

This brings us to the area of communication which floors more couples than almost any other, and that is sharing a spiritual dimension in marriage. Many Christian couples would pay lip-service to the great desirability of sharing this aspect of their lives together, and yet comparatively few actually do it. Oh yes, they may go to church together, they may even be involved in various forms of Christian activity together, but when it comes to praying and sharing spiritual experiences on a one to one basis, they back away. A group of a dozen couples were asked, 'How important is prayer in your marriage?' and they all replied, 'It's very important.' But when they were asked, 'How often do you pray together?' eleven out of the twelve couples replied, 'Hardly ever.'

Now praying and reading the Bible *together* is no substitute for our private and personal spiritual life. That must come first. But after that, standing together before God is a powerful bonding force in any relationship. The apostle John says, 'If we are living in the light of God's presence . . . then we have wonderful fellowship and joy with each other' (1 Jn 1.7). Now the word 'fellowship' means 'to share intimately and take part in' — in other words *communication*! So that verse could be paraphrased, 'If we are living in the light of God's presence . . . then we have wonderful communication and joy with each other . . .' Well, if that is true, why do we hesitate? Perhaps it is because of the condition in the first part of that verse, '*If* we are living in the light of God's presence'. Living in the light means that all the dirt, defeats and failures are shown up, and maybe we are not prepared to be honest and open enough with each other to allow God's searchlight to play over our lives when we are together. We put on a religious mask, even for our nearest and dearest, and the thought of taking it off can be very threatening.

If that is your situation, let me remind you of two important points that we considered earlier. Firstly, if God has forgiven you for all your failures, then you are indeed forgiven, and you can stand before heaven and each other without fear, recognising your imperfections but rejoicing in the remedy for them and relaxing in your acceptance of one another.

The second point is that any form of communication only happens when you actually try it. You may not find it very easy at first; you may not do it very well, but keep that ideal of wonderful joy and intimate sharing in front of you and take the first step by deciding what form of spiritual sharing will suit you. Then secondly, make it short, regular, achievable and real.

What is right and realistic for us?

Couples who have been brought up in a traditional church setting with a liturgy, where prayers are usually written down and worship is more formal, may feel anxious about embarking on extempore prayer, especially in front of someone else. If that is how you feel, don't worry. You can use written prayers or you can use the Psalms. From time to time, why not agree on what you want to pray for, and then pray together but silently, with one of you ready to say a final sentence and the Amen after a given amount of time? Perhaps you might move on to praying for certain subjects turn and turn about, with each of you just saying one sentence aloud and then holding the matter up to God in silence. Prayer is not a technique, it is talking to God and there is no universally correct and accepted way of doing it. Be yourselves, be natural and be flexible, and you will soon find out what is most meaningful for you both.

Communication with God means listening as well as speaking, and many couples like to read something helpful together before they pray. Deciding what this should be can be quite difficult if you are both following your own course of Bible readings in your individual devotional time and are perhaps reading something else with your children at bedtime or in family prayers, if you have them. If you try to take in too much during the day you can end up with spiritual indigestion! One possible solution is to use a book of devotional writings from preachers and teachers of the past to add variety (*Edges of His Ways** by Amy Carmichael is one of my all time favourites) and occasionally to take it in turns to share whatever has struck us from our own Bible reading earlier in the day. Again, there is no 'set' formula, but if we come to God together, genuinely wanting to communicate with him, we can be sure that he will not let us down.

Make it brief, achievable, regular and real

Many of us give up on our prayer and sharing time together because we are too ambitious! Tim was at theological college, and he decided to teach his wife at least some of what he was learning in his college course. So he announced that they would study together for two hours, three evenings a week. After the first week of New Testament Greek and studies in the minor prophets his wife dropped out of higher education! Keith and his wife felt that they needed to pray more, so they decided to follow the example of some well-known Christians whom they had read about and get up an hour earlier each day to pray at length together. What they failed to take into account was that Keith was widest awake at night, whilst Jill was a morning person. As a result they found that while Jill read the prayer topics aloud, Keith dozed off quietly and, by the time she had prodded him into consciousness, the baby was awake and crying. They tried changing to the late evening, but, whereas Keith was really reacting by then, Jill's engine was definitely slowing down. That experiment lasted three days! Success came when they decided on an achievable goal. They cut the time to 15 minutes, and prayed together immediately after the children were in bed and they had eaten their evening meal. Eureka! It worked!

So, if you have tried before and failed, do have another go, but don't set your sights too high at first. It is better to pray together regularly once a week and accomplish that, than it is to decide on an hour a day which, for you, is an impossible target (it may not be for everyone, of course) and find that you become discouraged and give up altogether. And do remember that you are not going through a ritual but meeting a real person. That makes all the difference!

Growing together

Praying and reading the Bible or devotional books together are not the only forms of spiritual communication available to us, of course. There is also the simple sharing of what God is teaching us or what we believe and why in ordinary conversation. This may proceed fairly smoothly when it is just a matter of imparting information. But if there are points of doctrine or practice about which we disagree, or areas of difficulty that we aren't prepared to admit to, for fear of appearing foolish or unspiritual, then communication can screech to a jarring and abrupt halt.

The other potential trouble spot that we don't always recognise is that spiritual growth, like any other kind, is slow and not always obvious from day to day. And people grow at different rates. Sometimes one individual reaches a point of understanding or meets with God in a particular way that his partner doesn't share at that moment. Now one of three things can happen as a result. The partner who is in a growth spurt may be able to share it with his wife with sufficient delicacy and tact to keep her from feeling inferior spiritually, and to enable her to understand and share it with him (it could, of course, be the wife who is in this position just as easily; the same rule of tact applies, only more so, because men are sometimes very touchy about being 'behind' their wives in anything). Or he can try to hurry her along to his point of view by argument or persuasion. Or he can keep quiet about the whole thing for fear of causing problems. Does that sound familiar to you? It is certainly part of my experience.

When our three children were pre-schoolers, Gordon was the leader of the teenage group at our church. I was more than happy for him to do it initially, but gradually the gloss wore off. The group grew and flourished; they had a coffee bar to which many youngsters from outside the church were attracted, and the leadership responsibilities began to take up so much of Gordon's time that he was out of the house more evenings than he was in. Exciting things were happening on a spiritual level too. Teenagers were meeting Jesus for the first time, and the Holy Spirit was moving in the lives of many of them in new and dramatic ways — but I was left out. We lived too far from the church for them to use our house for a base, and we had too many baby-sitting problems for us to get out together very often. Gradually I became more and more resentful about what I felt to be the general unfairness of life. I was angry with God because he wasn't blessing me in the same way as he was blessing everyone else (or so it seemed). I was angry with Gordon for being out so much — although I knew he couldn't help it, and he did try to involve me as much as he could — and I was angry with myself for being angry! The devil had a field-day and of course, our communication suffered because eventually there were things that we simply didn't talk about. It took quite a while to get that tangle sorted out, but from it we learned several important things —

1. THE PERSON WE LOVE BEST IS NOT ALWAYS THE RIGHT OR ONLY INDIVIDUAL TO HELP US WITH A SPIRITUAL PROBLEM

Many ministers and others who are heavily involved in Christian work find this — they can counsel everyone but their own wives (or husbands). As one of them said, 'When I get home at night, I don't want to hear about Beccy's spiritual problems too often — I've been dealing with that sort of thing all day. I want her support and understanding. And I'm really too close to her to see her needs objectively. Added to that, perhaps I'm a bit afraid, too, of preaching to her what she knows I don't practise! Of course we want to share our spiritual lives together. But if we have a real difficulty we don't feel it wrong to turn to someone outside our marriage for help.'

2. WE BOTH NEED TO HAVE OUR OWN PLACE WITHIN THE BODY OF CHRIST BUT WE ALSO NEED TO RECEIVE REGULAR SPIRITUAL FOOD TOGETHER

It is very easy to become a spiritual leech! If they have a family and are not able to go out with their husbands easily, many wives slide into the rut of staying at home because it's easier, and leaving their partners to attend meetings and become actively involved with the church (it can of course happen the other way around; in either case, it is counter-productive). They then expect their husbands to provide most of the spiritual in-put in their relationship, and feel hard done by and resentful when he becomes more mature as a Christian. We can't live life second-hand. There are times when we will go to things alone, of course. And hopefully, on these occasions, we will be able to share what we have learned afterwards. But don't abandon the principle of growing together. Yes, I know all too well the problems of finding baby-sitters, but it is possible for at least some of the time.

We have friends who both became committed Christians after they were married and had a family, and they were horrified at the way the church seemed to split couples up. 'When we wanted to go to the pub or the cinema in the old days,' said Ginny, 'we got a baby-sitter. We wouldn't have considered going alone. So why shouldn't we do the same now? We do go out alone to church things occasionally, but in our church we've abandoned "Young Wives" in the evening in favour of things that couples can enjoy together —and having tried it for a year now, we can recommend it!'

3. WHEN EITHER OF US IS ASKED TO TAKE ON A
   RESPONSIBILITY OR OFFICE WITHIN THE CHURCH, WE
   NEED TO DO SO ONLY AFTER COUNTING THE COST IN
   DISCUSSION AND PRAYER, AND FOR A SPECIFIED PERIOD
   OF TIME

In one survey of Christian marriages, the greatest stress factor that couples felt was placed upon their relationship was pressure of church responsibilities. There are some couples who virtually never see each other, so how can they hope to communicate or grow together spiritually? We need to be realistic. Of course, Christians both need to and want to be involved in bringing the good news about Jesus to the world around them. But if we are called to be married and have a family, then this is where we must consider our priorities in the allocation of our time. These relationships have a prime claim upon us, second only to our personal walk with God. We often become more preoccupied with what we do than what we are — God looks at things the other way around.

4. WE CANNOT DO THE HOLY SPIRIT'S WORK FOR HIM!

In this matter of spiritual growth and sharing, there is a temptation to say to ourselves 'God doesn't seem to be handling this situation very well; I can't see much change in my husband/child/friend — perhaps I'd better give him a helping hand.' Don't! It is the Holy Spirit's job to open the eyes of individuals to spiritual truth. Yes, we have to do our part; to teach children and to share what we know to be true for ourselves with other adults. But we can't bludgeon or nag people into the Kingdom of God (and this applies particularly if you have children or a husband/wife who doesn't share your faith), nor can we force growth until it is ready to happen. So we need to pray for and with each other; to share what we have discovered (remembering always that we are simply one beggar telling another beggar where to find bread — and then leaving him to find it) and ask God to set us free from envy, jealousy, pride or fear, so that we can be genuinely glad when those we love are blessed. After all, as long as we both remain 'united to him', both having a hand in the hand of God, we shall certainly reach our final destination together.

20: Come Help Change the World

'Be humble and gentle. Be patient with each other making allowances for each other's faults because of your love. Try always to be led along together by the Holy Spirit, and so be at peace with one another . . . Lovingly follow the truth at all times — speaking truly, dealing truly, living truly — and so become more and more in every way like Christ' (Eph. 4.2, 3, 15, LB).

Hilary got married at later than the average age. Her career took precedence over marriage plans for a number of years and she had climbed quite a long way up the ladder of medical research when she met Hugh. It was a whirlwind romance, and although Hilary had thought carefully about what she wanted in a husband in her more reflective moments, the excitement of falling in love at last blinded her to the fact that was quite obvious to all her friends — Hilary and Hugh were as different as the proverbial chalk from cheese.

Hilary's dreams of marriage didn't match up to reality, for although both she and Hugh were Christians, their temperaments, ambitions and ideas about life were incredibly different. Hilary was secretly horrified to discover that the man she had expected to lean on, look up to and be challenged by, was in reality a rather broken reed. Hugh was a kind and gentle person but, having come from a broken home, and with a lonely and very unhappy childhood behind him, he had many fears and emotional hangups which he hid, very successfully, from the outside world, behind a strong, silent and very efficient mask.

Hilary was clever and enthusiastic, ambitious and outgoing, and yet secretly longing to be cherished and protected. She had hoped for a 'soul-mate' with whom she could share everything; discussing, analysing, and arguing as she had been used to doing with her professional colleagues. Hugh communicated very little and arguments of any kind just shrivelled him up. She expected to have a husband who was better than her at almost everything (she read too much romantic fiction). The only things at which Hugh was noticeably more able than her were reading time-tables and cookery!

The first two or three years of marriage whirled by in a flurry of nappies, bottles and broken nights, as Hilary coped with their twin daughters, a home in a strange part of the country, and the absence of her career, as best she could. At first, the novelty of being a wife, mother and homemaker dulled the nagging feeling of disappointment and dissatisfaction, but one day, after yet another attempt to communicate with Hugh about their relationship had failed, she phoned her vicar in desperation for counsel and comfort.

'It was a most extraordinary thing,' she said. 'I was pouring out my problems when this picture came into my mind. I would hardly dare to call it a vision but it was a picture of such incredible clarity and colour that I lost the thread of what I was saying completely. In it, Hugh was walking up the path to meet me. But it wasn't the rather silent and withdrawn person I knew. He was glowing with life and happiness; laughing and reaching out his arms to a group of people standing nearby. And as I watched, God spoke to me with absolute clarity.

' "This is my beloved child," God said, "and this is how I see him. This is what he can become. I have called you into this relationship to minister to him and to communicate my love. That is the way I have chosen to heal and to help him. Together you can build something beautiful for me".'

That moment of vision transformed Hilary's outlook and ambitions for her marriage, and when she shared it with me, I felt both humbled and challenged. 'In my medical research,' she said, 'I had hoped to discover something to help mankind as a whole. Now I have a different goal because I've seen how important one individual is to God. No amount of time, effort or love on my part will be wasted if it can help Hugh to be that person that God wants him to become.'

The world is full of broken things — broken relationships, broken homes and broken people. And yet God's will for us is that we should be whole — mature, fulfilled, integrated and at peace with ourselves and each other. In his love, he offers us what we need; significance, acceptance and a purpose in life, and when we have grasped these things for ourselves, he asks that we should communicate them to other people — not en masse, but one at a time. There is no situation and no individual who is in too many pieces for God to put together again. So let's remember, as we try to use our communication skills to express his love, '*as one person, I may not be able to change the world, but with God's help, I can change the world for one person.*'

Postscript

The Prayer of St. Francis of Assisi

Lord, make me an instrument of Your Peace.

Where there is hatred, let me sow love,
Where there is injury, pardon
Where there is doubt, faith
Where there is despair, hope
Where there is darkness, light
Where there is sadness, joy.

O Divine Master grant that I may not so much seek

To be consoled, as to console
To be understood, as to understand
To be loved, as to love.

For it is in giving that we receive
It is in pardoning that we are pardoned
It is in dying that we are born to eternal life.

Bibliography

This list comprises all the titles referred to in the course of the book, which are followed by the sign*.

Amy Carmichael, *Edges of His Ways* (SPCK, London, 1955)

Edward R. Dayton & Ted W. Engstrom, *Strategy for Living* (Regal Books, Gospel Light Publ., Glendale, California, 1976)

Joyce Huggett, *Two into One* (IVP, 1981)

Pat King, *How Do You Find the Time?* (Pickering & Inglis, Basingstoke, 1982)

Alan Lakein, *How to get Control of Your Time and Your Life* (Signet Books, David McKay Co. Inc., 750 3rd Ave. New York, 1973)

Marcia Laswell & Norman Lobsenz, *No Fault Marriage* (Doubleday, New York, 1976)

Marabel Morgan, *Total Joy* (Hodder & Stoughton, London, 1976)

John Powell, *The Secret of Staying in Love* (Argus Communications, USA, 1974)

Michel Quoist, *Prayers of Life* (Gill & Macmillan, London-Dublin, 1963)

Edith Schaeffer, *What Is a Family?* (Hodder & Stoughton, London, 1976)

Gail Sheehy, *Passages* (Bantam Books, 1977)

Marion Stroud, *The Gift of Love* (Lion, Tring, 1981)

Marion Stroud, *The Gift of Marriage* (Lion, Tring, 1982)

Paul Tournier, *Marriage Difficulties* (SCM, no date)

This book has truly been a joint effort, and so many people have taken a share in it, that it is impossible to thank them all personally. Some have opened their homes and their hearts to me, sharing deeply personal problems and experiences.

Others have written their ideas down, loaned me books, or pointed me to other useful sources of information.

A special group of people have shown their love in many practical ways as they have prayed and encouraged me to press on, when the whole project seemed impossible.

To each one of them this book is dedicated — with gratitude.